T0049471

"Michael and Shaunti's impactful research will help you separate what really heats up your intimate life from what doesn't. If your sex life isn't all you dreamt it would be, discover your own path to transformation in this game-changing book."

—Toni Nieuwhof, author of *Before You Split*
and co-host of the *Smart Family Podcast*, and
Carey Nieuwhof, author of *At Your Best* and
host of the *Carey Nieuwhof Leadership Podcast*

"Intimacy is such an important part of a marital union. Fully researched and biblically sound, *Secrets of Sex and Marriage* is a great tool for any married couple to read together and grow closer in their intimate life. I highly recommend this insightful book to all married couples."

—Gary Chapman, PhD, author of *The 5 Love Languages*

"*Secrets of Sex and Marriage* uniquely identifies with the readers in their journey to a healthy marriage and sex life. Michael and Shaunti wonderfully blend helpful information validated by research with practical application. After forty-seven years as sexual therapists and educators, we learned useful new facts and found this a very enjoyable read."

—Dr. Clifford and Joyce Penner, clinical psychologist
and clinical nurse specialist; both certified
sex therapists; authors of *The Gift of Sex*

"A book like this only comes around every so many decades. This is a non-opinion book, a sound resource to guide both therapists and couples. The language is simple and rich with life examples. As therapists who work with minority populations, we cannot be more excited to share such a transformational tool."

—Jorge and Danisa Suarez, marriage counselors and
sex therapists; co-hosts of *Sexo Divino TV*

"The secrets are out! Feldhahn and Sytsma have mined the feedback of more than 5,300 individuals to provide the clearest picture of marital sexuality we've ever had. This book is an incredible gift to couples, families, the church, and the world."

—Christopher and Rachel McCluskey, bestselling authors of *When Two Become One: Enhancing Sexual Intimacy in Marriage*, co-founders of Professional Christian Coaching Institute

"As the pastor of a large multicultural church, I've counseled many people from all walks of life. . . . A great marriage is a universal desire. And so is a great intimate life. My friend Shaunti Feldhahn and Dr. Michael Sytsma have researched and created a quick-read book that will get you to both!"

—Miles McPherson, senior pastor of The Rock Church in San Diego and author of *The Third Option*

"Anything and everything that Shaunti and Jeff write we read and share with others. Their research and insights are always so practical and life-changing. This book . . . will bring life and hope to the very foundation of your marriage. Fasten your seatbelt and prepare for some real wow revelations!"

—Dave and Ann Wilson, hosts of *Family Life Today*

"Married couples reach out to Focus on the Family regularly seeking help with the sexual aspect of their relationships—which is why I'm especially thankful for this new book by Shaunti Feldhahn and Dr. Michael Sytsma. Through extensive research and their own keen insights into this important topic, Shaunti and Michael show couples that it's more than possible to achieve a mutually satisfying sex life that contributes to a healthy, vibrant marriage."

—Jim Daly, president of Focus on the Family

"This book is a gem! Writing succinctly and in an engaging style, Shaunti and Michael offer couples valuable insights and actionable steps to improve their marriage and their sexual relationship. I will definitely use this book with my clients and recommend it to friends!"

—Debra L. Taylor, marriage and family therapist
and certified sex therapist

"The secret is out! We read this book together and agree that Shaunti and Michael expertly share practical sex and marriage truths that every couple needs."

—Montell and Kristin Jordan, pastors of Master Peace
Church and authors of *This is How We Do It:
Making Your Marriage a Masterpeace*

"*Secrets of Sex and Marriage* is one of the most relevant marriage resources on the market. With eye-opening research on modern sex, biblical foundations, stirring real-life illustrations, and practical applications on every page, this book can bring renewal to any marriage both inside and outside the bedroom. Every couple (including us) can benefit from this book!"

—Dave and Ashley Willis, authors of *The Naked Marriage*
and hosts of *The Naked Marriage* podcast

"A lot of people guess at the What, Why, and How of sex. But guessing doesn't work. *Secrets of Sex and Marriage* wraps the authors' combined professional experience around solid new research that will put guessing aside and make way for a more intimate marriage and sexual relationship. Read it!"

—Ron and Nan Deal, Empowered to Love seminars, and
author (Ron) of *Building Love Together in Blended
Families* (with Dr. Gary Chapman)

"Using research you can trust, Shaunti and Michael invite couples to a greater level of understanding. . . . This book unlocks the prevailing secrets and misunderstandings that keep couples at odds with each other, inviting them to experience a new understanding, empathy, and pleasure."

—Gary Thomas, author of *Sacred Marriage* and *Married Sex*

"This book contains a tremendous combination of insight, research, and real-life practical help! Without question, it will inform, encourage, and instruct couples as well as those who minster to them."

—Dr. Juli Slattery, president and co-founder of Authentic Intimacy and author of *Rethinking Sexuality*

"*Secrets of Sex and Marriage* is real talk! We mean real talk—about the awkward and sometimes difficult conversations about sex, even in marriage. Whether you want to fan the flame of passion or spark a deeper desire for your spouse, this book is your go-to resource!"

—Apryl and Ozzie Ortiz, podcasters and founders of Strength & Dignity Life

"*Secrets of Sex and Marriage* is an eye-opening, useful, and much-needed tool for every counselor, pastor, and leader who works with marriages. . . . A must read!"

—Tim Clinton, EdD, LPC, LMFT; president of American Association of Christian Counselors; co-host of *Dr. James Dobson's Family Talk*

"Shaunti and Michael write with great wisdom and care. Biblically sound and evidence-based, [this book] is a trusted resource for pastors, counselors, and therapists who want to help couples in this sacred part of life."

—Ted Cunningham, pastor of Woodland Hills Family Church, Branson, MO

secrets of
sex and
marriage

Other Nonfiction Books and Resources by Shaunti Feldhahn and/or Jeff Feldhahn

Thriving in Love and Money

Thriving in Love and Money Discussion Guide

Thriving in Love and Money Discussion Kit

For Women Only: What You Need to Know about the Inner Lives of Men

For Men Only: A Straightforward Guide to the Inner Lives of Women

For Young Men Only: A Guy's Guide to the Alien Gender
(coauthored with Eric Rice)

For Young Women Only: What You Need to Know about How Guys Think
(coauthored with Lisa Rice)

For Parents Only: Getting Inside the Head of Your Kid
(coauthored with Lisa Rice)

3-in-1 For Women Only, For Men Only, For Couples Only DVD Study

Through a Man's Eyes: Helping Women Understand the Visual Nature of Men
(coauthored with Craig Gross)

The Male Factor

The Surprising Secrets of Highly Happy Marriages

The Good News about Marriage
(with Tally Whitehead)

The Kindness Challenge

The Life Ready Woman
(coauthored with Robert Lewis)

Made to Crave for Young Women
(coauthored with Lysa TerKeurst)

DEVOTIONALS AND BIBLE STUDIES BY SHAUNTI FELDHAHN

Find Rest: A Women's Devotional for Lasting Peace in a Busy Life

Find Peace: A 40-Day Devotional Journey for Moms

Find Balance: Thriving in a Do-It-All World

Find Joy: A Devotional Journey to Unshakable Wonder in an Uncertain World

FICTION BOOKS BY SHAUNTI FELDHAHN

The Veritas Conflict

The Lights of Tenth Street

secrets of
sex and
marriage

8 Surprises That Make
All the Difference

SHAUNTI FELDHAHN
and DR. MICHAEL SYTSMA

BETHANYHOUSE
a division of Baker Publishing Group
Minneapolis, Minnesota

Published by Bethany House Publishers
Minneapolis, Minnesota
www.bethanyhouse.com

Bethany House Publishers is a division of
Baker Publishing Group, Grand Rapids, Michigan

Printed in the United States of America

Library of Congress Cataloging-in-Publication Data
Names: Feldhahn, Shaunti, author. | Sytsma, Michael, author.
Title: Secrets of sex and marriage : 8 surprises that make all the difference /
    Shaunti Feldhahn and Dr. Michael Sytsma.
Description: Minneapolis, Minnesota : Bethany House Publishers, [2023] |
    Includes bibliographical references.
Identifiers: LCCN 2022029148 | ISBN 9780764239557 (cloth) | ISBN
    9781493439218 (ebook)
Subjects: LCSH: Married people—Sexual behavior. | Sex in marriage.
Classification: LCC HQ31 .F365 2023 | DDC 306.7086/55—dc23/
    eng/20220721
LC record available at https://lccn.loc.gov/2022029148

Cover design by Lucy Iloenyosi, NeatWorks, Inc.

Authors represented by Calvin W. Edwards

Baker Publishing Group publications use paper produced from sustainable
forestry practices and post-consumer waste whenever possible.

23 24 25 26 27 28 29   7 6 5 4 3 2 1

To the trailblazers
who have gone before us—
especially Dr. Douglas Rosenau,
who ran his race well.

contents

Opening Note   13

1. What We Want—And How to Get There   17

2. What Are Married Couples Up to in the
   Bedroom?   33
   *Why sex matters, and how knowing what is "normal" is half
   the battle*

3. What We See   67
   *Why an encouraging vision will illuminate your marriage even
   when the lights are off*

4. You Are Not Broken   83
   How embracing different types of desire opens up delight

5. "I Want You to Want Me"   105
   *How purposeful connection is even more important than
   desire levels*

6. Sexual Healing   131
What sex—and the process of getting there—says to our hearts

7. The Magic Touch   155
How a curious approach is a sexual superpower

8. Getting Started   171
Why real connection comes more from the right signals than the right moves

9. Love the One You're With   193
How a great response to disappointment can create a great relationship

10. A Higher View   215
Moving forward with what matters most

Acknowledgments 227

Appendix, *published online*
at secretsofsexandmarriage.com:
Our Methodology and Research Process 235

Notes 237

opening note

from sex therapist dr. michael sytsma

I avoid most books on sex.

I do read *a lot* of textbooks, clinical books, and professional journals on sex. But unless the author is trained in sex and sex therapy, books for the general public are written with the best of intentions but often filled with mythology, inaccuracies, and potentially harmful information.

Also, popular books cannot cover all the differences among marriages and individuals. Over decades of private practice, I have listened to thousands of sexual stories. Reading popular books about sex, I think of people who don't fit the concepts presented. Learning to be playful with your spouse sounds great—unless they are hypercritical, demanding, and the source of your trauma.

So I was hesitant when Shaunti and Jeff proposed we write a popular book together. I respect their work, have advised them over the years, and recommend several of their books to clients. But I lean toward crafting a three-thousand-page book addressing all the "but what if my spouse . . ." caveats. The editors broke the news that approach wouldn't work.

In the end, the thought of doing great marital-sex research and writing up the findings in a way that could enrich *most* marriages was irresistible. **But I must share a few cautions.**

First, because I have studied this subject for literally thousands of hours, many consider me an "expert"— but no one is an expert on *your* life or *your* marriage besides you and God. If something works for 97 percent of couples, you just might be one of the 3 percent. If something in this book doesn't feel right for your story, your marriage, or your spouse, it might not be. It will fit someone else. Just step around it.

Second, this book as a whole may not be right for you at the moment. Some couples want my help in their sex life but are *way* not ready to work on something that intimate. They may need to learn to better manage generalized anxiety or treat depression (both of which biologically short-circuit healthy sexuality). They may need to work on healing trauma. They might be in a marriage with an unhealthy power balance or a spouse who doesn't truly honor them. Other issues may simply need to be addressed first.

Therapy allows me to customize teaching and interventions to the individual stories in front of me. I can't do that in a book. To speak to the majority of people, some in the minority may feel sidelined. If that is you, we are sorry. It's not our hearts, but a limitation of the medium.

Bottom line: If you and/or your marriage are in a particularly difficult place, or if a particular situation doesn't apply to you, certain invitations in this book might actually be harmful for you. Please proceed carefully.*

That said, the majority of marriages are either reasonably healthy or can get there with a bit of work. Most spouses truly care for each other. If you are in this camp, we have worked extremely hard to bring you a book filled with practical help for growing one of the core arenas of marriage.

Please don't just read it and set it aside. Read it out loud to each other. Stop often to ask each other what you think. Lean in. Be curious. Talk openly. Discuss how what we are saying does and doesn't fit you and your marriage. Fight to make it great.

Thanks for the privilege of speaking into a sacred part of your life.

—Rev. Michael Sytsma, PhD, LPC, CST, CPCS

*For a further perspective, see my special note starting on page 211 and secretsofsexandmarriage.com for an article on how most marriages (including those in difficult places) can benefit from these efforts—even when extra care is needed.

what we want— and how to get there

Jackie and Trent were grinning like teenagers as they snuck down the hill to the pitch-black soccer field. It was 1 a.m., their young children were having a sleepover at Grandma's, and the couple was here to fulfill yet another promise they had made to each other twenty years before.

They started dating in high school and quickly felt certain they would eventually marry—but decided to wait until marriage to have sex. But they flirted about all the places they would do it once that day finally came. "When we're married," he whispered as they walked along a beach with friends on spring break, "we're going to come back and do it here." "When we're married," she challenged him, "I want to find a lonely mountain road, pull off into the trees, and do it in our car."

Now, after twelve years of marriage and three kids, they still looked young and tried to *stay* young by fulfilling those promises. Jackie had suggested this outing a mere hour before, so here they were, in the middle of the night, sneaking into a suburban park where he had issued such a challenge after a soccer game at age sixteen. They drove around the shadowy "Park closed" sign and giggled as they grabbed a backpack of supplies from the car, quietly shut the doors, spread a blanket on the soccer field, pulled on another blanket for cover, and got busy.

They didn't even hear the police car pulling up.

"You there!" The booming voice of an officer quickly interrupted what they were doing, causing them to jump and gasp. "Get up here!"

Mortified, Jackie and Trent pulled on their clothes and stuffed their things into the backpack. At least, Jackie was mortified. She was shocked to see Trent looking *amused* as he grabbed her hand and headed toward the police car and the two officers standing beside it.

The first police officer started with Trent, reading the information from his driver's license aloud so his partner could enter it on a computer tablet.

"Trenton Smith. 1234 Spring Drive." He finished reading the address and handed back the license.

Then he read Jackie's.

"Jackie Smith. 123—" He broke off. "Wait, this is the same address. Same last name." He looked up sharply into their faces, shining his flashlight more directly. "I thought you were college kids! You're *married*?!"

Trent, still grinning slightly at the officers—who looked about their age—said, "Yes, officer. We're both thirty-six. Married twelve years. Three kids."

"Dude!" As the second officer started laughing, the first officer's expression changed to one of inspired awe. "That is *awesome*! Respect!"

"We'll let you go with a warning." The second officer shut down his tablet. He gave Jackie and Trent a half salute as the two men slid inside the vehicle. "And our shift is about over. My wife just texted me that she is still up, and I do believe it is time to run on home myself!" Both grinning widely, the officers drove away.

THOSE AREN'T THEIR TRUE NAMES,[1] but that is a true story. When Jackie shared it with me, I (Shaunti) couldn't help laughing out loud, I loved it so much. Since then, whenever I have shared that anecdote with friends or at marriage conferences, everyone has the same reaction I did. There is a deep, instinctive feeling of *I want that!*

To be clear, people don't necessarily want to *do* what Jackie and Trent did! (For some, that would be uncomfortable rather than appealing.) Rather, what people are thinking is, *I want to have a delightful, playful, intimate life with my spouse!*

We are here to tell you that in the vast majority of cases—you can.

Every marital situation is unique. Some couples are starting from strength, others barely hanging on. But except for in some fairly rare situations, nearly every married couple can have the hope of a meaningful sex life for a lifetime. A sex life that helps create and protect a meaningful marriage.

A Very Different Approach

How can each of us get to that delightful, playful, rich, intimate life with our spouse? That is what this book is about.

But this will be a very different approach. Most resources on this topic focus on general sex-and-marriage enrichment. Although that can be quite valuable, this book is more specialized. It is co-written by an actual sex therapist with thirty-five years of clinical experience, and a social researcher with a twenty-year track record of uncovering simple and life-changing answers to the questions the average person wonders about.

This is not a "sex manual" trying to cover all the bases (so to speak). And you will not see stories like the above used to illustrate broad formulas or overly simplistic tips and tricks. A satisfying intimate life cannot be created by flirting in a certain way, trying spicy new ideas, or sleeping together under the stars to liven things up (although if that does it for you, go for it!).

Rather, our approach is based on **transformative understanding**—of our spouse and of ourselves. That is what *does* have the power to create a satisfying, lasting intimate life. Otherwise, although everyone *wants* great intimacy, we tend to pursue solutions that won't get us there *because we are focusing on the wrong things.* Instead, we need to have our eyes opened to simple but crucial truths many of us have not known or have been misunderstanding for years—truths about each other and about how our minds, hearts, and bodies work.

We need to have our eyes opened to simple but crucial truths many of us have not known or have been misunderstanding for years—truths about each other and about how our minds, hearts, and bodies work.

These fascinating realities, uncovered via painstaking research on normal couples, point to *real* solutions. So once we understand and apply them, we can have clarity instead of confusion, heal hurts, communicate so much better, and love one another well.

We hope this approach will make it easy for you to learn and talk about these things that we often don't talk about!

If any of you are thinking, *I can't believe I'm reading a sex book*, well, let me (Shaunti) tell you: I can't believe I am writing one! My husband, Jeff, and I have always been slightly embarrassed to talk about this topic—not just with others but even between the two of us—and we know we are not alone. So we will make every effort to address awkward topics with sensitivity, to make your own conversations easier.

The Eight Surprises

What are the little things that will make a big difference? Although there are exceptions to these patterns (more on that below), here are eight areas of confusion or misunderstanding—and the surprising truths from the research that will help us understand our spouse and ourselves and reach a new level of intimacy in marriage.

You may wonder...	The truth is...	Chapter
What is "normal" for a sex life, what are we missing, and how can I fix my spouse/myself and get where we want to be?	There is a wide range of "normal," and understanding some very simple truths can help us thrive.	2 – Normal
How do we fix our problems in the bedroom?	Creating a healthy intimate life starts with what happens in your mind, not with what happens in the bedroom.	3 – Vision
Why doesn't my spouse want me? / Why aren't they interested? – Or – Why don't I "want" my spouse in the way I'm supposed to?	Our culture has a male-centric view of what desire is, and what it means to "want" your spouse. In general, for men, desire leads to sex; for women, sex leads to desire.	4 – Desire Types
How can we get on the same page about how often we want to have sex? How can I and/or my spouse increase/decrease desire levels?	Even with desire differences, we are not as far apart as it might seem—which makes bridging the gap easier than we might think.	5 – Desire Levels
Why does my spouse go cold, shut down, pout, and/or pull away about sex? (Or the lack of it?)	Men and women tend to have different insecurities that often go unrecognized, and the process of sex can create hurt–or bring healing.	6 – Insecurity
Is this as good as it is going to get? What can we do to prevent sex from becoming rote, boring, or even marked by anxiety about whether it will be "good?"	To make sex more erotic and emotionally meaningful, curiosity and playfulness are more important than perfect technique.	7 – Curiosity
I thought something was going to happen tonight; how can I avoid this disappointment? – Or – I was just not in the mood tonight; how can I convey that without causing pain?	Having a comfortable way to signal and receive openness (or interest), in a way that is genuine to each of you, will create connection and prevent much pain.	8 – Initiation
How can I get my spouse to be more of what I need / fix disappointments / work with me on improving our intimate life?	Accepting that your spouse isn't everything you wanted lets you enjoy what you've got.	9 – Acceptance

Some Introductions

Since we'll be spending a whole book together, let us tell you a bit about us and the innovative research that makes this book unique.

About us

From Shaunti:

I'm not a therapist, pastor, or social worker. I always say that I'm just a semi-confused wife who happened to have an analytical background and unexpectedly became a social researcher and bestselling author on relationships.

I started out with an analytical graduate degree from Harvard University, then worked on Wall Street. In 2004 I researched and wrote the book *For Women Only*, which launched a series of research-based relationship books. Designed to uncover the little things that make a big difference, they have sold nearly 3 million copies in twenty-six languages around the world.

That research had always been conducted by me and my husband, Jeff, and our team. This book is different. For such a sensitive topic, Jeff and I knew we had to partner with someone with a long-standing specialization and national respect in the field of marital sexuality.

So we reached out to our longtime advisor, Dr. Michael Sytsma—whose PhD study, clinical practice, and graduate-level instruction of others have specialized in marital and sexual therapy—and began meeting with him weekly for the next three years. (We had to laugh at people's reactions when someone asked, "What did you do yesterday?" and we answered, "We went to see a sex therapist.")

My co-authoring the book with Dr. Sytsma—Michael— doesn't mean Jeff isn't involved. For the rest of this book, Jeff will be the silent partner. Even though his name is not on the cover, Jeff was there for every meeting, participated in all of the research, and his insight is woven throughout these pages.

From Michael:

By contrast, I *am* a pastor, professional counselor, and certified sex therapist, and it is an honor to bring my training and experience to this project.

Other than my role as a husband to my wife, Karen, and father to our two sons, my most important vocational role is pastoral. I am an ordained Wesleyan minister. While I served in a traditional staff pastor role for over a decade, most of my pastoral work has been in marriage ministry. I have invested over 30,000 hours caring for individuals and couples in counseling, mainly with sexual issues.

To this project I bring over 2,400 hours of professional education in sexuality and sex therapy, plus a scary amount of reading and research in textbooks and professional journals preparing lectures to train others. In the early 2000s I partnered with some great friends to found Sexual Wholeness, Inc., where we train and certify Christian sex therapists. Over the years, I have trained hundreds of pastors and therapists in sexuality as a professor for ten seminaries around the country and in other venues around the world.

Earning a marriage and family therapy PhD from a tierone research university infected me with the research bug, and I have continued researching various aspects of marital sexuality. For this project, one of my primary goals was to help translate important clinical and academic knowledge into the more accessible language of this book.

About the research

This book is based on decades of rigorous research and experience via three avenues: extensive research and experience from Michael's thirty-five years of clinical practice, pastoring, doctoral studies, and leadership in the marital sexuality field; input from Shaunti and Jeff's nationally representative prior research with more than 35,000 men, women, and teenagers over twenty years; and our groundbreaking joint research study, the Marriage Intimacy Project. (If you aren't interested in the research details, just skip the shaded section. Also, note that you can see our data—and many other resources—via our website, secretsofsexand marriage.com.)

The Marriage Intimacy Project

Over three years, the Marriage Intimacy Project (MIP) pulled together a fairly large team (ten staff members, two professional survey companies, and dozens of partner organizations and individuals) to rigorously gather and analyze input from more than 5,300 individuals. This included surveys and anonymous interviews (usually conducted via a video with the couple's camera off and using fake names; "Farm Boy and Buttercup" and "Wanda and Vision" were two favorites).

The hard costs were funded by a $120,000 grant from two silent donors to whom we are very grateful.

We conducted four main surveys—two primary, and two specialized. While most surveys use a "convenience sample" of whoever can be found to complete them (often recruited through social media or existing networks), the two primary MIP surveys were generally nationally representative for factors such as gender, age, race/ethnicity, religious attendance, geographic area, orientation, and education level. This makes the Marital Intimacy Project a unique and powerful study.

Specifically, the Matched Pair Survey (or MPS) included 501 married couples (1,002 individuals married to each other). This is one of the largest nationally representative matched-pair sex surveys of married couples *ever* completed and was accomplished with the help of Shaunti and Jeff's long-time partner company Decision Analyst.

In addition, the Married Individuals Survey (or MIS) is a nationally representative sample of 1,097 married individuals (data from only one spouse) completed in partnership with Dynata, another prior survey partner.

For our third and fourth surveys, we surveyed 250 church-going couples at six diverse church events across the country and 801 mental health professionals recruited through the American Association of Christian Counselors.

You can see more in the Methodology appendix at our website, including how we worked to ensure this content would both be practical and meet professional research standards.

As You Read . . .

As you walk through the chapters to follow, here are a few important points to keep in mind. (Then, if you want to go further, you can find many resources for couples and leaders at secretsofsexandmarriage.com, including an assessment, a streaming course for couples, resources for those in need, church small-group curricula, and tools to help pastors, churches, counselors, and other leaders.)

- *Our findings will not apply equally to all readers.* The key findings are true and helpful for most couples in most cases—but if 75 percent of spouses on a survey felt a certain way, that means 25 percent didn't. We will make generalizations for the sake of speed and clarity, but every marriage is unique, as is every individual. You might be the one in four who doesn't fit the generalizations. Use these findings as a starting point for discussion and mutual understanding. We encourage you to read the book out loud to each other, a bit at a time, and stop to discuss.

- *This book addresses issues faced by the large majority of couples and cannot cover highly specialized and/or abusive situations.* As Michael mentioned in his opening note, this book is directed to the overwhelming majority of couples who care about one another and are dealing with common needs and concerns. Although we care deeply about the uncommon situations and the most hurting marriages, we simply do not have the space to address them here. So if you are dealing with a specialized situation—for example, a challenging neurodiverse marriage or medical issues that make sex physically difficult or impossible—use wisdom and seek counsel in how or whether to apply these findings. And if you are facing a serious concern such as marital abuse or repeated sexual violations of the marital vow, please do not try to apply these findings, and instead get help from an experienced professional right away.

▧ *We will include a faith-based perspective.* Although the research is rigorous and representative across the board (among people of all religious beliefs and of none at all), our resources are widely used by churches and faith-based organizations. We personally come at life from a Christian perspective, which you will see reflected at several points in this book. We hope you will find these truths valuable even if you are coming from a different perspective. Also, this book is designed to be more practical than theological—but sex itself will be far richer if a couple rightly understands it as sacred and created for a sacramental purpose (see chapter 10).

> This book is more practical than theological— but sex itself will be far richer if a couple rightly understands it as sacred and created for a sacramental purpose.

▧ *We include a science-based approach to common gender differences.* Although many findings were not particularly gender oriented, several were indeed related to common misunderstandings and differences between men and women. Discussion of gender can be controversial, yet multiple studies reveal gender differences, even if shaped by social construct. These differences are particularly obvious around sex and reproduction and often showed up in our data.

- *Our data included input from all sexual orientations; however, this book focuses on mixed-sex couples.* According to the Census Bureau, same-sex couples comprised 0.97 percent of marriages and 1.5 percent of households in 2019.[2] Non-heterosexual orientations in our data set were represented at a slightly higher number, but were still, comparatively, a small sample. It appeared that some of our findings would apply to non-heterosexual couples and some would not. Exploring those details moves beyond the scope of this book.[3]

- *This knowledge can help even if you are working on your marriage alone.* Although no one wants to feel like the only partner trying to work on the marriage, we have seen many troubled relationships transformed by the power of a one-sided choice. Your spouse is still accountable for their choices, but you cannot change your spouse; you can only change yourself. This means loving and pursuing your spouse in the ways you can, and trusting God to work in the ways you can't. Your spouse will have to decide what they will do; you are not responsible for that. But you *can* give yourself the best chance of heading in the direction you want to go if you follow God's charge to do what *you* can do.

Getting Started

So are you ready to dive in? The ability to get to a delightful, playful, meaningful intimate life isn't limited to a lucky few who have just the right mix of temperaments, equal sexual desire, or the ability to communicate perfectly. Remember our opening story? Jackie and Trent are just a normal couple. They don't have it all figured out. They have a mismatched desire for frequency (she wants more than he does) and normal marital issues (he works a lot more hours than she wants him to). But they also know how important their sexual relationship is. So they keep working toward intimacy—with all that means—and experience the delight of being together. You can too.

what are married couples up to in the bedroom?

why sex matters, and how knowing what is "normal" is half the battle

THE SURPRISE: There is a wide range of normal, and understanding some very simple truths can help you thrive.

D oes sex really matter? I (Shaunti) recently had this conversation with one of the many medical professionals I saw during my recent, unexpected treatment for breast cancer. We got to talking about how certain cancer treatments can reduce libido, and I told her about our research for this book. She asked if she could take off her professional hat for a moment to discuss what we'd been finding. Her usual polished manner dropped away, and she exclaimed in some exasperation, "I just don't understand why sex is so important! I've been married a long time, and we are way past our newlywed phase. Does sex really *matter* so much to a marriage?"

As you will see in the data to follow, the answer is clear: Yes, it really does.

But *why* is sex important to a marriage?

We'll address deeper reasons in chapter 10, but for now, think of it this way: In a standard car engine, the constant friction of moving parts would destroy it quickly without oil. In many ways, just as oil is the lubricant of an internal combustion engine, the sexual relationship can be the lubricant in a marriage. (We promise we aren't trying to make a double entendre with this metaphor; it just works!) Neurochemical shifts and positive feelings help reduce relational friction. A protective sense of togetherness and powerful connection can be created. The causes of friction still exist (two different people doing life together), but the sexual relationship ideally helps buffer the rough edges.

The problem, of course, is that sex doesn't always work that way. In some marriages, the sexual relationship doesn't act as the lubricant it is supposed to be. In others, it becomes a cause for distress. Or in some seasons, everything is working just fine and then some upheaval—a new baby, different job, medical issue—seems to drain the oil. So how do we acknowledge the difficult seasons and situations and still get as close as possible to the ideal God designed?

One of the simplest, yet overlooked solutions is to be sure we are operating based on accurate information. (And fair warning: As you might imagine, there's some sensitive language ahead!)

Trying Hard in the Right Areas

The couple sat across from me (Michael) for their first session. The problem? "He's too quick." In other words, he was climaxing before they wanted him to. After trying a host of "fixes" that didn't work, they turned to shame, blame, and attacks. He was convinced there was something wrong with him. She was convinced he was purposefully withholding pleasure from her.

But when I asked him, "How long do you typically last?" he reported somewhere between ten and fifteen minutes of active intercourse. She said she needed twenty minutes to climax. *I think I see the problem.* How long did she think he should last? "Until I am ready, so we can climax together." They both believed mutual orgasm was the goal.

Like many I work with, this couple had spent years trying hard in the wrong areas. They'd been working to achieve mutual pleasure and intimacy based on false beliefs and misinformation. They didn't know that the average male reaches orgasm in 5.4 minutes[1] of intercourse[2] (this husband was actually more than double the average) or that the average female takes fourteen minutes to reach orgasm[3]—almost three times as long as the average male. Climaxing together may be great when it happens but is usually a poor goal.

Armed with the right information, they were able to develop realistic goals and remove the patterns of shame, blame, and unhealthy beliefs—which allowed them to relax into playfulness and intimacy.

Most of us care for our spouse and are trying hard. But when we are operating under wrong assumptions, we are trying hard in the wrong areas. We may be pursuing fixes that will never work or putting effort into things that simply don't matter to our spouse as much as we think they do. Worse, our efforts may even be *hurting* our spouse or the marriage.

> Most of us care for our spouse and are trying hard—but often in the wrong areas.

We have to shift our focus to what's accurate and true. We love our spouse and are trying to create a great sex life but have probably picked up many wrong assumptions that lead us to wrong solutions. We may not recognize that we have skewed expectations about sex from media, culture, or a hundred other sources. Many of us even have significant gaps in our knowledge about sex, blind spots, or flat-out misinformation that are getting in the way of the great intimate life we want.

It's no wonder we experience challenges, confusion, and hurt on a topic so rife with misunderstanding—especially when it is one we might be embarrassed to talk about!

It's time to set the record straight, answer some questions—and hopefully give you some transformational knowledge and reassurance at the same time.

Setting the Record Straight

To some degree, every chapter in this book is about replacing wrong assumptions with correct ones. Let's start with some of the most foundational, and tackle three very common, inaccurate ideas many of us have about the state of our sexual unions, what really matters—and what really doesn't. Knowing the truth may naturally change what you want to do—sometimes quite dramatically—as you pursue a thriving intimate life. (Note: All the data below—and in the rest of the book—is available in detail at the Research section of our website, secretsofsexandmarriage.com.)

NORMAL

> **WRONG ASSUMPTION #1:** We are not normal. (Especially, my spouse is not normal!)
>
> **THE TRUTH:** You are probably more normal than you think—and so is your spouse. Many sexual issues are common.

When Jeff and I (Shaunti) speak at marriage events, people often privately approach us with sensitive questions. They ask about low or high sexual desire, what's normal for frequency of sex, what to do about menopause, trauma, erectile dysfunction, porn use, and all sorts of other concerns.

Concerns you may have too.

Since Jeff and I aren't therapists like Michael, there are some technical questions we can't answer. But we quickly learned that it doesn't seem to matter much. The technical answer often doesn't reduce the questioner's subtle anxiety anyway. What does is much simpler: the strong reassurance that what they are dealing with isn't unusual. That they are normal, that help is available, that they are not alone.

All of us need that reassurance in some way. Since sex is one of the few areas where we rarely compare notes with even our closest friends, it's easy to feel that we are one of few couples dealing with something. Yet *every* marriage deals with sexual issues and concerns. Everyone has ways that our hopes for what sex *would* look like don't measure up to what it *does* look like.

Thankfully, most problems are not as intractable as they may look and do not have to hurt a marriage. And there are many simple steps that *can* help our intimate lives meet our most important expectations. Further, the reason we can tell most people "You are normal" and "Your spouse is normal" is that there is a vast array of normal!

It is important to note that by "normal" we primarily mean typical or common. That doesn't always mean that something is okay or optimal. Hiding things from your spouse might be normal and quite common, but it's not okay. And it's fixable.

It's the same with sex. Many sexual patterns are normal and not problematic or destructive at all; they are just the way that couple is. But as noted earlier, some common struggles *are* destructive and need to be addressed. However, they don't need to be accompanied by the shame of feeling alone in those struggles!

Because you are not alone. In most cases, millions of people are dealing with the same issues. With the right information and motivation, we can address them. (Although we'll touch on various issues in the chapters ahead, because this book is not a sex manual, we recommend looking at one for specific topics of interest. You might start with *The Gift of Sex* by Cliff and Joyce Penner or *Celebration of Sex* by Douglas Rosenau.)

Let's briefly touch on three of the areas where it is common to ask, "Are we normal?"[4]

How often should we be having sex? What is normal?

Sex therapists avoid the question of normal frequency of sex. The correct answer is always "it depends." It depends on age of the spouses, age of the marriage, number and age of their children, physical health, impact of trauma, health of the marriage, etc. There is a wide array of normal frequency, from never to daily.

Similarly, a normal amount of sex also doesn't equal what "should" be happening. If you want things a certain way and believe the majority of people have it that way, it can be tempting to use that to pressure your spouse with "we should too." Not only is this not effective, it is inaccurate. Even if 70 percent of your community has a pet, it doesn't mean you should. Maybe you travel all the time or are allergic to pets. Being one of the 30 percent might be right for you. When it comes to sex, you or your spouse might have a very good reason for not being part of the statistical norm. Use "normal" as a conversation starter, not as a standard.

> You or your spouse might have a very good reason for not being part of the statistical norm. Use "normal" as a conversation starter, not as a standard.

So what *is* the statistical norm? For couples who are actually having sex (excluding low-sex/no-sex couples—more on that in a moment), the average frequency for all couples falls right at 1⅓ times per week (four times every three weeks). Interestingly, there was no statistical difference between regular churchgoers and everyone else in average frequency, but churchgoers were almost twice as likely to be having sex, period, than those who rarely or never attended church.[5]

Look at how spread out the answers are (see below): 23 percent of couples have sex less than once a month (or not at all), 28 percent report one to three times per month, 29 percent report one to two times per week, and 15 percent say three to six times a week. Then, of course, there is the robust 4 percent of the population who have sex daily or

How often are couples having sex?

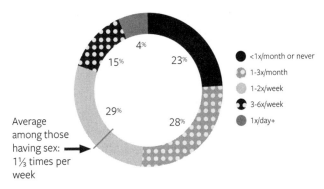

4%
15%
23%
29%
28%

- <1x/month or never
- 1-3x/month
- 1-2x/week
- 3-6x/week
- 1x/day+

Average among those having sex: → 1⅓ times per week

Source: MPS, n=501 couples

more. (When we refer to "having sex" we mean all sexual activity, not just intercourse.)

Even if you and your spouse are having little if any sex, you are also not the only ones. Yet this is an example of where normal is *not* necessarily healthy or ideal. As noted, 23 percent of this nationally representative population is having sex rarely or never (9 percent) or less than once a month (14 percent). In

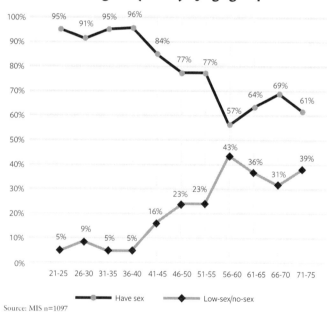

Having sex (or not) by age group

Source: MIS n=1097

Not surprisingly, the percentage of low sex/no-sex marriages increases with age.

the sex-therapy field, these "low-sex/no-sex" marriages (which is what we will call them) are often considered "sexless" marriages and typically pair with other problems.

Low-sex/no-sex marriages are also much more likely to be among older couples. On the Married Individuals Survey (MIS),[6] among those over age sixty, more than one-third (36 percent) of couples are not having much or any sex, compared with 27 percent of those age forty-one to sixty, and just 5 percent of those age forty or below. (See graph.)

Looking at the *reasons* for sexlessness, 77 percent of those in low-sex/no-sex marriages reported reasons that appeared to be physical and unavoidable, while 23 percent shared reasons that appeared to be based on choices or relational issues.[7] Thankfully, though, even unavoidable physical factors don't make a lack of sex inevitable.

What type of sex is normal?

There is a wide array of sexual practices out there. That doesn't mean they are all healthy (more on that below), but it is likely that whatever you two are doing, others are doing too.

A common question in this category is about the prevalence of oral sex. Nationally, among couples having sex, 78 percent of spouses practice oral sex (37 percent most of the time and 40 percent some of the time[8]), and 22 percent said they rarely or never do.[9] (The numbers were similar for churchgoers.)

That said, there were substantial differences between men and women in terms of who *enjoyed* giving and receiving oral sex. Fully 82 percent of men said they enjoyed receiving it, while only 38 percent of women enjoyed giving it. And 60 percent of women said they enjoyed receiving oral sex, while a *higher* ratio of men—70 percent—enjoyed giving it.

It is also clear from the research and clinical experience that even when a spouse might not naturally "enjoy" giving oral sex, many do take delight in giving delight to their spouse if their *spouse* enjoys it! As always, the key is to use this as a starting point for conversation—including talking about how frequently you want to engage in a given behavior and what specifically you enjoy about it.

What if sex sometimes doesn't work well? What if my spouse doesn't "work right"?

We subconsciously think sex is supposed to always work well and be a source of total connection. Thus, there must be something wrong if we're having a tumble in the sheets and are also partly distracted. ("Oh! I forgot to send the permission slip in for the field trip!") Or we think we must be not so great at the process of engaging our spouse if their mind is wandering like that. We may think we are unusual—or our spouse is—if there is pain, lack of enjoyment, or inability to climax.

These types of concerns and hiccups will happen to almost everyone. For example, many people are hoping for pleasure—

even more so, for their *spouse's* pleasure—but also have a bit of tension about whether they or their spouse will "get there." In fact, as you can see from the chart, 31 percent of women and 9 percent of men say they only occasionally *do* get there—and sometimes don't at all.[10]

How frequently do you have an orgasm during sex?

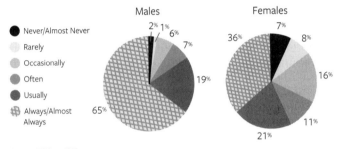

Males

Females

Never/Almost Never
Rarely
Occasionally
Often
Usually
Always/Almost Always

Source: MPS, n=1002
Percentages do not total 100% due to rounding.

Our bodies are *not* always intuitive. Especially in seeking good sex. Many men, in particular, appear to be slightly perplexed by how their wife is put together.

Remember: Once you know the real issues, you can pursue the right solutions. A few common misunderstandings are worth debunking.

First, many people think intercourse is enough stimulation for most women to climax. But for roughly 40 percent of women, it isn't; they require something *other* than intercourse in order to get there, and clitoral stimulation doubles the chance of orgasm.[11] And yet half (49 percent) of men and women on the MIS survey didn't know that.

At one marriage retreat, a discouraged thirty-five-year-old husband approached Jeff with the concern that his wife sometimes took more than forty-five minutes to climax, and sometimes didn't climax at all. He was discouraged because "I just can't, you know, stay hard that long." He had no idea that although his wife might be *enjoying* intercourse with him, her body probably required some sort of stimulation of the sensitive clitoral area to experience orgasm. (One study found that some of this was structural: The greater the distance between the vaginal opening and the clitoral glans, the less likely that intercourse can lead a woman to climax.[12]) We should note that in this sort of situation, there might be a host of other issues involved—but sometimes the solution can indeed be this simple.

Second, people tend to brush off the existence of sexual pain. Please don't. If you push through the pain, your body is likely to tense up and cause *more* pain. In our study, 12 percent of men and a whopping 32 percent of women feel pain at least every third time they have sex.[13] (And 58 percent of women have pain occasionally.) Yet 40 to 50 percent of women with chronic pain don't seek help.[14]

Sexual anatomy is complex and often poorly understood even by physicians. Pain can occur in a host of tissues, organs, and nerves and be caused by an even larger number of factors including birth control, neurological or musculoskeletal problems, inflammation, disease, genetics, psychosocial issues, and many others. When women do seek help, it often takes four to nine visits with medical professionals to accurately diagnose the pain.[15]

That said, we are dramatically improving our understanding and treatment of sexual pain and can usually do something to help. So if sex often hurts, please seek that help. And if your doctor's advice is to "just have a glass of wine before sex," get a new doctor. If after a talk therapy session your counselor tells you the pain between your legs is "vaginismus" caused by an idea a man put between your ears, get a new therapist. At best, those giving this advice are incompetent at dealing with sexual pain.[16]

Stop having sex that hurts, seek out a specialist who will do a thorough evaluation, and work with a multidisciplinary team to address your pain. (See our website for resources, including a list of specialists.)

Meanwhile, take this time to discover other ways to pleasure each other.

What other things can we do?

Millions of couples face common issues that may make intercourse challenging. But that does *not* mean they cannot share pleasurable sexual time together. In fact, making sex all about intercourse and climaxes is likely to be *counterproductive* over time—both spiritually and physically.

Sex is ultimately designed to bring you and your spouse together in one-ness. When *that* is the focus, the climaxes are put in the right perspective: They are great, but they aren't the *goal*. If we have tunnel vision about intercourse or even genital stimulation, what happens when things don't work as well as we want—for example, if the wife experiences dryness as she hits peri-menopause, or the husband has erectile issues? It is easy to default to a sense of futility and to back off on sex. Don't!

We can still have great sexual pleasure without intercourse. Think of two teenagers making out in the back seat of a car, who have decided they will not have sex or genital touch. They can still be *powerfully* aroused and even climax, right? That same thing can still happen, years down the road, when she begins to have dryness or he begins to have erectile issues. Exploring all the options for erotic, arousing connection may even be a *solution* to certain issues. For example, a wife may be having vaginal dryness, but quite often, when her husband gets creative, the arousal is *so* much higher that there's less dryness!

Consider this frank advice leading sex therapist Dr. Debra Taylor[17] shared with us:

I always recommend that you work with professionals to address any issue that makes intercourse difficult—vaginal dryness because of menopause, erectile difficulties, a health issue that inhibits orgasm, and so on. But as you do, don't stop sharing sexual time together! Often couples are so focused on the penis, vagina, and intercourse that they stop paying attention (or never discover!) the many areas of the body that are arousing—the lips, mouth, nipples, inner thigh, back of the knee, labia, clitoris, to name just a sample. Be curious; be creative. You both have hands and mouths— you have a variety of options to explore together that can bring pleasure, connection, and closeness.

Sometimes, something as simple as adding an excellent lubricant can help (as long as you are not bypassing a deeper issue that needs to be addressed). When we think creatively, it opens up all sorts of options.

> **WRONG ASSUMPTION #2:** Having consistent sex—or not— doesn't really impact the marriage
>
> **THE TRUTH:** Regular sexual intimacy with your spouse really matters to the marriage.

As mentioned earlier, a regular sex life *does* matter to marriage. Now, this does *not* mean that one must engage in regular sexual intimacy regardless of what is going on in the marriage!

In some marital situations (beyond the scope of this book), it is vital to refrain until sex is emotionally and physically safe for both partners. (If you have not read Michael's Opening Note on page 13, please do so before you go further into this book.)

Also, as we unpack in chapter 5, "duty sex" is destructive for the spouses and the marriage. In addition, what constitutes a "regular" sex life will look different to different couples—and it will be a lot easier for some couples than others. Thankfully, by thinking creatively, the vast majority of couples can overcome their obstacles and engage in sexual intimacy in a meaningful way.

Here's one key reason it matters: Couples who are in low-sex/no-sex marriages (having sex less than once a month) are much, much more likely to be struggling in many other ways in their marriage. And couples who are having more sex are far more likely to be thriving.

Those trends are especially clear when we look at how happy each couple is with how often they have sex, accounting for both partners.[18] As a baseline, 43 percent of couples are happy with how often they have sex, 33 percent are sort of "meh" (in the middle), and 24 percent are unhappy with their frequency. (Most low-sex/no-sex marriages are in the latter category.)[19]

But when we look at how happy each group is in *marriage*, the results are stunning. As you can see, among couples who are happy with how often they have sex, 94 percent are also happy in their marriage. Among those who are "meh" about their frequency, 70 percent are happy in marriage. And among those who are *unhappy* with their frequency, only 35 percent are happy in marriage!

NORMAL

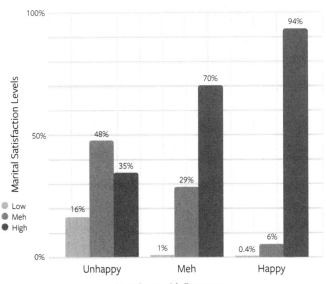

Marital satisfaction
by couple frequency satisfaction

Marital Satisfaction Levels

- Low
- Meh
- High

	Unhappy	Meh	Happy
Low	16%	1%	0.4%
Meh	48%	29%	6%
High	35%	70%	94%

Happiness with Frequency

Source: MIS, n=1097

94% of couples who are happy with the frequency of sex are also happy in marriage.

Considering the *vast* scope of issues that can impact happiness in marriage—parenting, jobs, in-laws, money, anxiety, work hours, and on and on—it is dramatic that this one factor of sexual intimacy is so highly correlated with marital happiness. But then again, if sex really is the oil that lubricates the marriage engine, this only makes sense.

One important note: We don't know how much of this correlation is because sex leads to marital happiness or because being happy in marriage makes you more likely to have sex. It is probably both. More research is needed to investigate this and many other correlated factors identified in our study. For the rest of this book, note that we do not yet know which correlated factors are *causing* a certain result, and which are merely related in some way. Either way, working hard as a couple to improve your sexual intimacy will improve skills and overall marital functioning that spills into improving other arenas of marriage.

As one wife described it on the survey, "I crave the closeness of sex with him. It feels sacred. When we don't have sex, I feel the disconnect; when we do have sex, I feel like we can work through anything together." Or as a husband put it, "The longer we go without sex, the more distant I feel we become. Being sexually active with my wife makes me feel so much closer to her."

Even more encouraging, having sex is correlated to another issue that impacts marital happiness. Many people today (28 percent on our survey) deal with clinically significant anxiety, depression, PTSD, and other mental health issues and are at higher risk of being less happy in their marriage as a whole.[20] *Except*, it turns out, among those who are having regular sex in their marriage! People with mood disorders who are having sex are more than *twice* as happy in their marriages as those not having sex. And among those having sex, the number of those unhappy in marriage is *tiny*.[21] (See page 54.) As one psychologist exclaimed when he saw those numbers, "So much for an *apple* a day!"

Now, keep in mind that having a relatively regular sex life at all seems to matter more than frequency. Even among the many couples who are sort of "meh" about how often they engage (for example, if one partner is fine but the other wishes there was a bit more action), the vast majority are still very happy in their marriage.

Sex isn't the be-all and end-all of a marriage. But being dissatisfied with sexual frequency is correlated with being dissatisfied with the marriage overall. We must take it seriously that a spouse who is unhappy about how often they have sex is *ten times more likely* to also be unhappy in their marriage.

Since it makes such a difference, what leads to being happy with frequency? Although the answer will of course depend on what matters most to each couple, three factors are common.

NORMAL

Relationship of Mood Disorders and Sex to Marital Satisfaction

Couples Having Sex

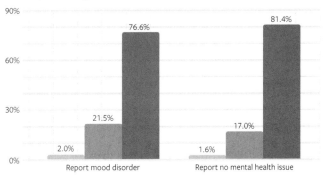

Marital Satisfaction:
○ Unhappy ● Moderate ● Very Happy

Low-sex/No-sex couples

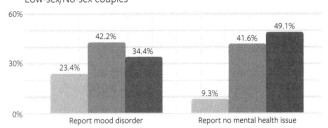

Source: MIS, n=1064.
Compares those with mood disorders only (n=269) to those with no reported mental health issues (n=795).

Those with mood disorders who are having sex are more than twice as happy in their marriages as those with mood disorders who are not having sex.

First, a couple is much more likely to be happy with how often they have sex if they are having sex once a week or more. Of such couples, 62 percent are happy with their pattern, compared with only 25 percent of those having sex one to three times a month! Among all those having sex less than once a month, only 9 percent are happy with their frequency as a couple.

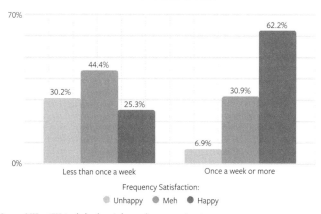

Those having sex once a week or more are more satisfied.

Frequency Satisfaction:
Unhappy   Meh   Happy

Source: MIS, n=782 (excludes those in low sex/no sex marriages)

And contrary to what it may feel like to a spouse in a low-sex/no-sex marriage, if one partner is unhappy with the frequency, the other most likely is too.[22] (More on that in chapter 5.)

That said, the unhappiness factor in a low-sex/no-sex marriage wasn't universal. We did see many couples who—for all sorts of reasons—could have little or no sex yet had created a wonderful relationship. We'll discuss the lessons we can learn from that group in chapter 9.

Second, a couple is more likely to be happy with frequency if they have roughly similar levels of desire for sex. Among those who report equal or similar desire, 82 percent of couples are happy with how often they have sex.[23] But the happiness level drops to only 18 percent for those marriages where one partner has significantly higher or lower sexual desire than the other. Much more on this—and what to do about it—in chapters 4 and 5.

The **third factor** we will cover below: **whether the partners can communicate well about sex.**

All of this is a wake-up call for spouses who think having little or no sex isn't a big deal. It appears to be a *very* big deal. And although there are many, many reasons a couple may be living in a low-sex/no-sex marriage, the good news is that most such couples can still find ways to be intimate—even if it doesn't look quite like they expected. A good resource to help get restarted is *Restoring the Pleasure* by Cliff and Joyce Penner.

> **WRONG ASSUMPTION #3:** We have a difficult time talking about sex, but that's okay. After all, actions speak louder than words.
>
> **THE TRUTH:** Actions may speak louder than words, but without the words, you may not be getting as much action.

NORMAL

When couples come into my (Michael's) therapy office stating, "We are having trouble communicating about sex," my first thought is, *You are communicating just fine. You just don't like—or you're misunderstanding—what the other is saying!*

Everything we do is communication. You can't *not* communicate.[24] Imagine that you and your spouse go to bed; you turn off the light, your spouse reaches over to brush a sensitive area, and you pull away slightly. Message sent and received.

The question isn't whether we are communicating, but rather whether we are communicating what we want to in a way that will achieve what we're hoping for. For example, you may have merely wanted to say, "I need some sleep," but your spouse heard, "I don't like you. Don't touch me."

This is one of the main reasons actually *talking* about sex is so important. No one is a mind reader. (*Did my spouse just move out of reach because they are still mad about that argument earlier, or because that particular touch didn't feel good?*)

The problem is that most of us don't talk about sex as well as we think we do. For example, 49 percent of our survey-takers initially claimed to be in the best communication group, saying, "We talk about sexual issues whenever we need to, without any awkwardness or difficulty." But then nearly half (45 percent) of *those same people* answered other questions that instead placed them squarely in the "liar, liar, pants on fire" cohort. For example, saying that it was definitely not easy to talk about what they wanted with sex, or that they would *not* want their hesitant or embarrassed spouse to talk to them!

Once we looked at how couples handle communication *in practice*, it appears that just 27 percent can talk about sex well, without awkwardness or difficulty, while 73 percent cannot—they either talk only awkwardly or simply avoid talking about sexual issues at all because it is difficult or won't get them anywhere. [25]

Or even, as one highly representative wife put it, "I sometimes avoid uncomfortable conversations because it might affect the mood later." But this doesn't have to be a selfish desire. As one husband told us, "There are things I sometimes wish I could say, but they are not as important to me as her feelings are."

Most of us need to take a candid look at whether we really do talk *well* about sex when we need to. As one self-reflective wife said in response to the awkwardness question above: "I don't know if it is necessarily awkward to talk about sex, it's just not something we sit and have a conversation about. Well, actually . . . maybe that's because it is awkward to sit and have a conversation about."

The research was clear that whether we can talk about sex well with our spouse—or not—has profound implications for our marriages and intimate lives. Here are just a few.

People who are able to talk about sex with their spouse have significantly more sex. The reverse is also true: People who find it awkward or difficult to talk about sex—or avoid

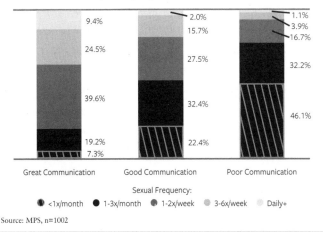

Sexual Frequency by Communication Level

	Great Communication	Good Communication	Poor Communication
Daily+	9.4%	2.0%	1.1%
3-6x/week	24.5%	15.7%	3.9%
1-2x/week	39.6%	27.5%	16.7%
1-3x/month	19.2%	32.4%	32.2%
<1x/month	7.3%	22.4%	46.1%

Sexual Frequency:
● <1x/month ● 1-3x/month ● 1-2x/week ● 3-6x/week ● Daily+

Source: MPS, n=1002

People who talk about sex well are happier with the frequency of sex.

doing so altogether—have much less sex. On our survey (MPS), 74 percent of those who had great communication had sex once a week or more, while just 45 percent of those who had reasonably good communication had sex that often, and just 22 percent of those with poor communication had sex that often![26]

The initial implication is clear: If you want to have more sex, start by learning how to talk about sex well with your spouse.

People who talk about sex well are also far more happy about the frequency of sex as a couple. Remember how important a couple's happiness with their frequency was? Well, 61 percent of those who had great communication about sex were happy with their frequency—compared with only 6 percent among those with poor communication![27]

Most important, people who talk about sex well are also far more likely to be happy in their marriage than those who do not. On our survey (MIS), those who could talk about sex well were much more likely to be on one of the highest rungs of marital happiness (89 percent!) than those who talk only awkwardly or with difficulty (74 percent) or avoid talking about sex altogether (62 percent). Even among couples having little or no sex, those who can talk about the topic are much more likely to be happy in marriage (67 percent) than those who don't (just 39 percent).

Remember that even among those very unhappy with the frequency of sex, more than one-third *were still happy in their marriage*. And many of those were the better communicators.[28] More research is needed to determine whether talking may compensate in some way for the lack of sex—perhaps because those who can talk well about sex also appear more generous in what they assume about their spouse's motivations toward them.[29]

Talking clearly matters. And learning more about each other and how sex works is a good foundation for it. One husband explained, "In the past, I'd have held back talking about stuff because we were both uncomfortable. But then I decided just to learn more about her and how her body worked and what I could do better. That gave me hope that I could figure things out if I just asked her."

Conversely, we set ourselves up for disappointment when we allow shyness or other concerns to keep us from talking. One person on the survey confessed, "I do hold back, but it's because I don't like to talk about sex. I wish my spouse would understand already what my needs are." As we all know, it is unfair to our spouse—and ourselves—to expect them to read our mind. And it is not in our self-interest! One woman on the MPS confessed that because she suffers from vaginal dryness, she is "scared of painful sex"—but because she also finds it very difficult to talk to her husband about sexual things, he may have no idea *why* she is avoiding it.

What a difference it would make if she could share the *real* issue with him and they could together go on a quest for a real solution. (They exist!)

Okay, we might ask, but what if—like 55 percent of those on the survey[30]—we're holding back because we're concerned about our spouse's reaction or worried about hurting their feelings?

Remember the principle that you can't *not* communicate. What you want is probably being communicated—or miscommunicated—in some way. For example, a fairly common miscommunication I (Michael) see happens when a husband is feeling distant from his wife and presses harder to be intimate as a way of saying *I feel totally disconnected from you, and sex would help me feel close again*. But because he's not actually saying that directly, what she may hear is: *He's just horny and wants to use my body—he doesn't want* me. The two spouses *are* communicating—they are just hearing the entirely wrong things.

Imagine if he were able to say, out loud, "I miss you. I don't like not feeling close to you. That's why I'm hoping to be intimate with you." And if she were able to say, "But every night you're gaming with the guys instead of hanging out with me! I need to feel close to you *outside* the bedroom first."

If we are going to talk about sex and intimacy well, we have to understand what to talk *about*. Because tensions over sex often aren't about sex per se but about a host of other factors running under the surface. Much of the rest of this book is aimed at helping you understand all of that, so you can connect well about the real issues, talk about them together, and build a more intimate relationship.

> Tensions over sex often aren't about sex per se but about a host of other factors running under the surface.

So What Do We Do?

At the opening of the chapter, we mentioned how we need to replace bad assumptions with good ones, so we can try hard in the *right* areas.

The first step to accomplishing that is to examine the three wrong assumptions in this chapter. Which do you recognize in yourself? What might you need to do as a result?

For example, do you need to consider whether your spouse's once-a-week desire for sex might be just as normal as your daily desire, and stop subconsciously assuming your spouse is deficient? Or perhaps you quietly realize, *Hmm . . . maybe my spouse is right to be concerned that we haven't had sex much in the last three months.* Maybe you recognize that you've been way too unconcerned about your spouse's pain and should encourage them to address it instead of downplaying it. Or do you need to start *talking* about sex willingly instead of with avoidance, embarrassment, or anger?

The second step is to ask your spouse to examine the same list. Have them share what they believe is most important for *you*! If you both are willing, read this book out loud to each other—pausing often to discuss what applies and matters most to each of you.

As you talk, be willing to hear your partner and discuss options without defensiveness or blame. Feelings of fault or failure may exist, but joint problem-solving won't happen if you are just venting anger or overly defensive about things your partner needs you to hear. If you two struggle with communicating calmly and positively (about *any* topic), consider consulting a counselor or working through a program that can help.[31]

Every couple will deal with different needs and issues; the most important step is being willing to examine them. The tools at secretsofsexandmarriage.com, especially our streaming course for couples, can help you increase your knowledge and understanding about *your* marriage, your intimate life, your spouse—and yourself.

The Little Things Do Matter

You might think that these seemingly minor actions—reassuring ourselves that we are not alone, talking about sex, and so on—would not make a big difference. But they do.

Several years ago, a couple came into my (Michael's) office. They were experiencing an issue that was causing immense heartache and pain in their sex life and eroding the heart of their marriage. After several sessions, they felt they were making progress and the issue was no longer putting their marriage at risk, so we ended therapy.

Here's the thing: *I never learned what the issue was.* And it didn't matter. I didn't need to know, because, as we have said before, *our issues around sex are rarely about sex.* In this case, the couple grasped what too many never do: They simply needed to figure out how to connect well, to talk with compassion and empathy rather than anger, and to see each other's hearts as they discussed what was running under the surface.

Truly, you are not alone. For the vast majority, these simple shifts—trying hard in the right areas—will make a big difference.

NORMAL

what we see

*why an encouraging vision will illuminate
your marriage even when the lights are off*

THE SURPRISE: Creating a healthy intimate life starts with what happens in your mind, not with what happens in the bedroom.

n 1999, researchers at Harvard University conducted the now-famous "Invisible Gorilla" experiment.[1] In a video, six people in black or white shirts passed basketballs back and forth, and viewers were asked to count how many times the people in white shirts pass the basketball.

Most viewers counted the passes properly. But half of them missed the fact that someone in a gorilla suit walks through the middle of the swirling players, faces the camera, thumps his chest, and walks off screen. If we haven't been primed to look for it, many of us might miss it too. When the video asks, "Did you see the gorilla?" half of us think, *Wait, what gorilla?!*

We missed what was most important.

A short documentary about the project described how researchers, using eye trackers, found that many people looked right at the gorilla for a full second and still didn't notice it. "Looking isn't the same as *seeing*. We have to focus attention on something in order to become aware of it."[2]

What You Focus on Is What You Will See

It is a crucial neuroscientific principle: What you focus on is what you will see. And what you see changes everything about how you respond to your spouse—since it is what you are responding to!

If we want a thriving, encouraging intimate life, we can't miss the gorilla. The encouraging, healthy patterns and truths that will build us up in our sexual relationship with our spouse *are there* to be noticed and applied. But so too is the temptation to focus on the swirl of the day and the stuff that simply doesn't matter as much.

A Mindset Shift

Let's look at six common mindset shifts that will make a difference.

MINDSET SHIFT #1: From problem to vision

It is easy to focus on what's not meeting our expectations. After all, that's why couples typically reach out for help—for desire discrepancies, the impact of trauma, conflict over practices, body parts not working the way people think they should, and so on. Yet ironically, an intense focus on the problems will only snarl things up and won't result in healing.

Picture what happens when a car accident causes a traffic jam on the highway. Traffic can be backed up for miles as drivers slow down to get a look at the problem, but as soon as you are past the wreck and are looking forward to where you are going, you speed up again and everything flows.

It works the same way in marriage—and is especially important with the sensitive issues of our sex life. If we want a hopeful, encouraging marriage, we have to shift our focus forward and be vision-oriented—what good future are we aiming for in our sexual relationship?—rather than simply tackling each problem in turn.

One of my (Michael's) most important homework exercises is to invite couples to create a sexual vision. Not just to say, "Here's how often we want to do it" (although that's fine as one point), but to flesh it out. How often do you want to cuddle? Do you want playful sex, erotic sex, functional sex, etc., or what is an ideal mix of each? What are ideal practices? Essentially, what will be fun, intimate, connecting, and healthy for you as a couple? Use that as the goal toward which you aim!

One of our most common and most inaccurate subconscious feelings—which applies to everything in marriage, not just our intimate life—is *My spouse doesn't care about me.* When we are hurt by our spouse (as all of us will be), we have a tendency to believe negative things about their intentions toward us. And usually, we see the motivations we most fear. *My husband said he was sorry, but it was only to stop the fight.* Or, *My wife doesn't really appreciate all I do.*

With sex, we might believe, *If my spouse really cared about me, they would want to have sex more.* Or conversely, *My spouse cares more about sex than about me.*

In all cases, the subtle internal belief is this: *My spouse doesn't really care about me or what I need.*

Those negative interpretations of our partner's intentions usually are quite wrong. Although there are some sad exceptions, most people care deeply about their spouse—even in the most troubled marriages. In research for an earlier book, *The Surprising Secrets of Highly Happy Marriages,* Jeff and I (Shaunti) found that out of 1,261 people surveyed, only 9 of them—0.7 percent!—had stopped caring. The rest—99.3

percent—loved their spouse and wanted the best for them. Even in the most struggling relationships, 97 percent still deeply cared.[3]

Now, sometimes an unintended cycle of hurt has taken on a life of its own and does need to be broken. In a marriage where the spouses truly care about each other, outward negativity often stems from emotional pain and not from a lack of love or a desire to hurt. But that negative response nevertheless does hurt the other spouse, who then responds from *their* emotional pain, and so on in a chain reaction.

For example, a husband might feel beaten down by a wife who sounds critical—and not realize that some of her manner arises because he has been emotionally unavailable and has left her feeling abandoned for years. Or a wife might feel the tension from a husband who gets verbally angry or withdrawn—and not realize that some of his manner arises from years of feeling derided. We are imperfect people, and we can sometimes be selfish or thoughtless. But that doesn't mean we don't *care*. And if you want a happy marriage, *you have to let yourself believe your spouse cares*. Which is usually the first step in arresting the negative cycle and creating a positive one instead.

When it comes to sex, believing a negative narrative is far more toxic to the marriage than our actual sexual difficulties. In my (Michael's) PhD dissertation, I found that the difference in how much sex spouses wanted didn't predict much distress. The greatest predictor of marital distress related to sexual desire differences was whether the high-desire spouse *believed something wrong* about the thoughts and feelings of the low-desire spouse! (For example, incorrectly believing that "they never want to have sex with me.")

> When it comes to sex, believing a negative narrative is far more toxic to the marriage than our actual sexual difficulties.

Thus, healing a hurt in our sex lives doesn't come primarily from tackling the technical problem (such as the gap in desire), but from eliminating the inaccurate belief! For example, rather than thinking, *My spouse only cares about their own needs*, someone might tell themselves, *My spouse may not know how to show it, but they may actually care more about my sexual pleasure than their own.* (Which, in fact, is usually true![4]) Or, rather than assuming, *My spouse only wants to give me a back rub because they want to get lucky—not because they care about* me, switch the assumption to, *My spouse may be wanting to connect with me sexually, but it is* because *they care about me.* (Which also is usually true![5])

All this said, some marriages are a tragic exception: One or both spouses are not operating out of goodwill and are instead abusive or controlling. But in most cases, hurtful behavior stems from a different dynamic.

> **MINDSET SHIFT #3:** From seeing "bad heart" to seeing "bad skill"

I (Michael) often ask a struggling spouse to consider this: Do your spouse's hurtful actions stem from a bad heart? Or bad skill? Because there is a big, big difference. A husband or wife may be poorly skilled in their ability to love their spouse well—but, thankfully, skill can be taught. So the question is, can you focus on their heart while they are learning the skill?

One woman's husband was indeed emotionally absent and empathically clueless. We were working on his unhealthy and painful behavior. But on her side, she had also become damagingly critical. I invited her to a different perspective: "I know how hard this is for you. But can you focus on his heart instead of how he is acting, and respond with *that* in mind?" They had a preteen son, and I asked her to consider whether she would respond with the same level of harshness to her son for similar behavior. She said, "Of course not, he's just a kid."

I said, "In other words, when you are confronted by poor behavior on the part of your son, what you're thinking is 'I've got a good kid, and he doesn't know exactly how to handle things yet and needs to learn.' Right?" I pointed out that we don't crucify our kids because of lack of skill, and it isn't helpful to do that to our spouse.

The hard part comes, of course, when someone really does have a bad heart. Because if someone is truly abusive, selfish, and not willing to love their spouse, that is very difficult to overcome and they're not safe to be with in the meantime. Thankfully, that situation (which requires specialized help) is rare.

Early on I worked with inpatient adolescents with serious behavioral and psychiatric problems. My supervisor once told me, "There are three kinds of kids admitted to this hospital. Mad kids, sad kids, and bad kids. In five years I have yet to meet a bad kid." I've since seen that dynamic every day with marriages in my therapy office. In my thirty-five-year career, I have probably seen about six people with a bad heart. Not six percent—six *people.*

Everyone else who hurts a spouse—which is all the rest of us—is dealing with varying degrees of bad skill.

Don't get me wrong: Bad skill *must* be addressed. Not long ago, I was talking to a husband who needed to temper his intimidating anger and relate in a healthy way with his wife. I told him, "You want me to help your wife understand how much you crave physical intimacy. But right now, it would be *unethical* for me to ask her to open herself up to you. You aren't safe. Until *you* learn to protect her heart, *she* has to." There are occasions when we need to establish boundaries and wait to resume a sex life until a partner's skill improves.

Are developmental or other such issues contributing?

We should also note that bad skill is sometimes exacerbated by certain significant developmental, personality, neurodiverse, or mental health issues. This might be one reason a study found that only about 38 percent of adults with Asperger's and other high-functioning autism live with a romantic partner.[6]

Also, a notable percentage of the married population—28 percent in our MIS survey (which may have overlap with the above group)—deals with common mental health issues such as anxiety, depression, and trauma. These also can lead to behavior that might be interpreted as a lack of care, when it is actually a lack of capacity in that moment.

In all such cases, it is crucial to shift our mindset so we allow for the possibility (or probability) that our angst stems from our spouse's lack of capacity rather than what feels like a lack of care.

MINDSET SHIFT #4: From "my spouse is dissatisfied with my imperfections" to "my spouse finds me and my efforts appealing, regardless"

Another critical wrong belief is the notion that our imperfections are a turnoff to our spouse. When we are insecure—about our naked bodies, our sexual abilities, our efforts to pursue our spouse—something in us thinks our spouse must be dissatisfied with us as well. It is a common fear, and usually completely unfounded.

As just one of many examples, look at the charts here and consider how tentative we are about our naked bodies, compared with how much our spouse *doesn't* want us to hide! Nearly half (48 percent) of those on the survey said they felt self-conscious about their spouse seeing them naked;[7] they worried their spouse would be turned off by their imperfections.

True or false? "I have been self-conscious about my body/my spouse seeing me naked (for example, getting out of the shower) / Worried they might even be a bit turned off if they see me as I truly am, with all my imperfections."	Total	Men	Women
That statement is definitely/somewhat true	48%	37%	58%
That statement is not very/not at all true	52%	63%	42%

Source: MIS, n=1052, heterosexuals only. Question/answers paraphrased.

Conversely, what do you think about seeing your spouse fully naked (for example, with the lights on during sex, or getting out of the shower)? Which statement is most true of you?	Total	Men	Women
I take delight in/want to see my spouse naked even with their imperfections	73%	85%	62%
I don't really care/not turned off by their imperfections	24%	12%	36%
Prefer not to see, because of imperfections	2%	3%	2%

Source: MIS, n=1052, heterosexuals only. Question/answers paraphrased.

Yet the vast majority (73 percent) of survey-takers—*the same people!*—said that they themselves *wanted* to see their spouse naked. And nearly all the others (24 percent, who were predominantly women) said they didn't care either way—but emphasized that they were not turned off by their spouse's imperfections. Just 2 percent said they were indeed turned off.

And what about those who are worried that their efforts to pursue sex might be awkward or clumsy? Similarly, 73 percent of those who said their spouse's efforts fit that category usually found those efforts endearing—and most of the rest (18 percent) said they were not bothered by them. (The main caveat was the many who said their spouse's uncertain efforts were appealing "as long as what they are doing isn't something I've repeatedly said I don't like.")

Clearly, we need to give *ourselves* as much grace as we give our spouse. So don't hold yourself back. Let this truth free you up—for example, to have sex with the lights on, and to allow yourself to try new things that might feel a bit fumbling at first. You'll get better with practice!

MINDSET SHIFT #5: From "are we allowed to?" to "what is healthy for us?"

When I (Michael) speak at a church, marriage seminar, or retreat, one of the top questions I'm asked is, "Can we _____?" Are we "allowed" to do this or that as part of our sex life?

"You're asking the wrong question," I typically respond. "You're assuming an external rule—or lack of one—is going to bring clarity and solve the problem. It cannot do that. This is about the heart, not about techniques and body parts. So look at the heart as you and your spouse decide together what is healthy for the two of you."

> Look at the heart as you and your spouse decide together what is healthy for the two of you.

Simple guidance comes from a foundational biblical directive about sex: "Marriage should be honored by all, and the marriage bed kept pure."[8] The word translated "pure" is the Greek word *amíantos*, which means "free from that by which the nature of a thing is deformed and debased, or its force and vigor impaired."[9]

So a simple test question is, does this practice remove any force or vigor from our marriage or sexual intimacy?

Anything that does so is hurting your hearts and is bad for you as a couple. This practice could be perfectly fine for another couple but if it makes you or your spouse feel uncomfortable or upset, it is robbing your marriage bed of force and vigor. If this practice is a cause for contention or hasn't really been *mutually* decided upon, or if one party is making the other feel guilty for not "getting with the program," then it is robbing the marriage bed of force and vigor.

This doesn't mean everything a couple might agree to is okay. We can defile what God has made holy.[10] Certain practices are corrosive to the marriage bed. For example, in my clinical experience, bringing a third party (including imagery) into the bedroom is always eventually damaging and is inconsistent with Scripture.[11]

Another way of getting at the principle is to ask: How would both of you feel afterward? Anything sexual that doesn't feel good afterward (emotionally, physically, relationally) *for both of you* isn't "good sex," no matter how it fits one spouse's fantasy or how intense the climax is.

Similarly, be cautious of any solo practices that can turn your heart away from your spouse and rob your marriage bed of force and vigor. For example, erotica or porn use may seem harmless to some, and yet fantasies about someone other than our spouse dilute the sacredness and distract our hearts—which is likely to be corrosive. Just as important, erotica and porn can set up expectations that will eat at your intimate life and the pleasure you find together.

As one female counselor told me (Shaunti),

When a woman catches her husband using porn, her awareness that it is happening can change how she views her marriage.

A lot of husbands don't understand that it can have a long-term effect. And it can set up subconscious expectations that are really damaging. Extensive porn use simply changes his view of what sex should be. And it's not just guys. Porn or romance novels can skew expectations for women just as much.

This topic has so many angles that it goes beyond what we can properly address here, but if this is an area of need, there are many resources to help both of you.[12]

Finally—and just as important—we've talked a lot about the concerns here, but don't just focus on those! Just as some behaviors would steal from you, there are others that will bring you closer, bring one or both of you great delight, and bless your marriage.

MINDSET SHIFT #6: From pursuit of pleasure, to pursuit of connection—of which pleasure is a byproduct

With such a wide variety of what is normal, it's really quite remarkable how often media portrays what is *not* normal! The beautiful people onscreen are always hungry for sex and have sex up against walls, on tables, in hot tubs, and never have issues with distraction or disappointment. Is it any wonder that we may have a skewed view of sex and question what we are missing?

We've also been conditioned to assume that the *goal* of sex is pleasure, culminating in a mind-blowing climax. As we will discuss in the final chapter of this book, God clearly designed sex for pleasure, but it is richer than just pleasure. If your goal is powerful pleasure, you might have only okay sex; but if your goal is intimate connection and oneness, then great sex is more likely to come along with it.

VISION

Steps to Take

Two crucial steps will help clear the way for far more encouragement in our intimate lives.

First, consider the principle that what you focus on is what you will see. Have you been missing something particularly important or encouraging about your spouse or your intimate life because you've been so focused on either the swirl of day-to-day life or the concerns around you? Ask yourself what positive "gorillas" you might be missing! Write down at least three that come to mind. Commit to noticing them—and, if appropriate, affirming your spouse for them—daily.

Second, we've covered six key mindset shifts in this chapter. Regardless of what your spouse does or does not do, which do *you* need to grapple with? Do you need to confront your tendency to believe something less than generous about your spouse's motivations in your sex life? (*He is only attentive when he wants to get lucky; he only cares about himself.* Or, *Since the kids came along, she just isn't inter-ested in me.*) Is there an insecurity you need to deal with to be more open in the bedroom? Is there something you can do to protect the force and vigor of your marriage bed?

Identify at least one mindset shift and commit to work-ing toward it.

Having a Good Eye

Both science and Scripture have much to say about the over-whelming importance of a right focus.

The Bible calls this having a good, or heathy, eye. Jesus said, "The eye is the lamp of the body. If your eyes [the things you seek out to look at, what you focus on, what you see] are healthy, your whole body will be full of light. But if your eyes are unhealthy [if you're focusing on the bad], your whole body will be full of darkness. If then the light within you is darkness, how great is that darkness!"[13]

How do we retrain our eye? In a terrible season of perse-cution, the Apostle Paul commanded the Christians in the ancient city of Philippi to "Rejoice!" He also provided a prescription for *how* to accomplish that: "Finally, brothers and sisters, whatever is true, whatever is noble, whatever is right, whatever is pure, whatever is lovely, whatever is ad-mirable—if anything is excellent or praiseworthy—think about such things."[14]

4

you are not broken

*how embracing different types
of desire opens up delight*

THE SURPRISE: Desire tends to work differently for men and women. In general, for men, desire leads to sex, while for women, sex leads to desire.

Jim invited me (Michael) to breakfast so he could get to know me before referring couples to me. I showed up in a marketing mindset, glad to talk to a community leader. Then he said, "The real reason I want to meet was to ask you a question."

Quick shift to therapist mode.

He launched in. "Isn't there some kind of cream I can slap between my wife's legs so she will want me more?"

I remember thinking, *I know what needs to be slapped, and it has nothing to do with cream.*

His question was *wrong* on so many levels—but also a signal of one sneaky, damaging belief about sex and desire. One that prevents us from intimately connecting and enjoying each other in the way we are looking for. A belief that saturates our culture and isn't held just by Jim.

And it has to be debunked before we can go any further.

The Big Myth

Consider how sex and desire are portrayed in everything we see around us. For example, in the average movie or TV show, both partners look at each other eagerly, start kissing, and go from zero to sixty in three seconds. Before you know it, the clothes are off and they are in bed.

There was a surge of desire, and they did something about it.

Although we know media portray sex in over-the-top *situations*, we tend to think that the overall *pattern* is just how sex works. You feel desire, get aroused, want to have sex, and go at it. That's just what sex *is*.

Here's the problem: That's "what sex is" for less than half the population—and is a far more common pattern among men than among women. But since most of us don't know that, we subconsciously expect sex to work a certain way and get frustrated with each other—or ourselves—when it doesn't. We might think, as Jim did, *There's something wrong with my spouse. How can I "fix" them so they respond to sex the way I do?* Or we think, *There's something wrong with* me.

The reality is: There are not one but *two* primary desire patterns, and these are often (although not always) gender related. With various exceptions (covered below), desire tends to work differently for men and women. In general, for men, desire leads to sex; but for women, generally, *sex leads to desire.* This overall understanding is the key to unlocking immense freedom and enjoyment. We are simply *built* differently. Your spouse is not broken—and neither are you.

A Primer about Desire

Let's dive into a primer on the *real* facts about desire every married individual should know, and how this should change your approach to each other, for the better.

FACT #1: There are different types of desire

One of our most damaging misunderstandings is not realizing there are different patterns of desire. The type we see on TV—the "I'm hungry for sex with you" feeling—is called *initiating desire.*[1] That seems to be our image of the "right" kind of sexual desire. But that type of desire describes only four in ten people![2] And in only 5 percent of couples do *both* spouses work that way.[3] In other words: In 95 percent of marriages, at least one spouse does not normally feel desire and pursue it!

> In 95 percent of marriages, at least one spouse does not normally feel desire and pursue it!

Yet because most couples don't know different patterns exist, the absence of initiating desire is often seen as wrong. While sometimes there can indeed be something wrong (for example, when a medication is reducing desire), most of the time there's nothing wrong; the person simply experiences a different type of desire.

The second primary type of desire is called *receptive desire*. The key characteristic is that the person is open to sex but, for various reasons, simply doesn't think about sex as often and feels desire in a different order than the person with initiating desire.

If we think of it like a car, initiating desire is like the vehicle being in drive: Even if the driver isn't pressing on the gas pedal, the car is being drawn forward—in this case, toward the goal of sex. Receptive desire is like a car in neutral; the car is waiting to be dropped into gear and pulled forward.

Desire combinations among married couples	
Both spouses have initiating desire	5%
One spouse has initiating desire, one has receptive desire	53%
Both spouses have receptive desire	29%
One or both have resistant desire	13%

Source: MPS. n=916

DESIRE TYPES

Most of this chapter will deal with these two primary types of desire. However, we should mention a third type that applies to a smaller number of people (7 percent) and signals the need for more specialized attention: *resistant desire*.

A full discussion goes beyond the scope of this book, but briefly, resistant desire is more like a car with the parking brake on—or even in reverse. It is not the same thing as lacking interest or having a low level of desire (which might be compared to having low or no fuel in the car). It is an active resistance to sex.

As with the other desire types, people with resistant desire experience it with different intensities: from an unwillingness to engage, to a consistent avoidance of sex (or situations that could lead to sex), all the way to a fear or hatred of sex. And as with all matters of sexual desire, resistant desire is complex. Sometimes it is unhealthy in itself, but it could also be present for a purpose that must be understood (for example, an unsafe or demanding spouse).

For the resistant-desire spouse, the message "just choose to have sex" is typically counterproductive. Yet because this relatively small percentage of individuals impacts 13 percent of all marriages (since in nearly all such marriages, just one partner is resistant), it is essential to address the issue. Given the importance of sexual connection to your marriage and your own well-being, if you or your spouse find yourself in the resistant category, we advise that you seek out a professional who can help unpack the core of the resistance. (See secretsofsexandmarriage.com for referral resources and other help.)

For the vast majority of couples (82 percent), though, the issue is simpler: One person has initiating desire, the other has receptive desire—or both have receptive desire. So let's turn off the TV and set aside the latest story about how sex works, and see how these two types of desire play out in real life.

FACT #2: Desire can be felt in a different order

In one of our early, informal surveys, we invited people to respond to this query: "If you could ask a sex therapist ONE QUESTION, what would it be?" The most common question among men and many higher-desire women went something like this:

"Why isn't my spouse as interested in sex as I am?"

This is more than an academic question. As one forty-something husband put it:

> My wife assures me that she finds me attractive and is very in love with me, but her interest in making love is about 25 percent of my interest level. How can this be, if she genuinely still finds me attractive and desirable? She offers many explanations for her lower level of interest (long day, perimenopause, just tired, etc.), but are these just nice things she is saying to cover up her finding me less attractive and desirable? I'm exhausted with trying to figure her out and with trying to be more attractive.

Much of this type of angst goes away once both partners realize that what is often seen as a lack of interest is actually a physiological difference that makes sexual desire *felt in a different order*.

For those with initiating desire, the *feeling* of desire tends to arrive up front. You feel desire for sex, get aroused, and get busy.[4] This timing is felt more than twice as often among men (59 percent) than women (24 percent).

DESIRE TYPES

But among those with receptive desire, the feeling of desire is experienced later in sexual engagement, not at the beginning. This person usually decides to get sexually engaged, begins to get aroused, views the arousal as positive, and *then* feels the sense of sexual desire their initiating partner felt from the very beginning. That feeling can arrive five or ten minutes into the sexual play.

Many people have heard the microwave versus Crock-Pot analogy of sex, where one partner is ready quickly and the other takes some time. But what most of us haven't realized is that taking some time isn't just a matter of warming up. The physiological process of desire is occurring in almost the reverse order.

In other words: Because of their physiological makeup, most of those with receptive desire must make a *decision* to get sexually engaged, and then a few minutes later are glad they did. This is *not* a matter of someone choosing to have sex even if they actively don't want it (which could be wounding). Rather, this occurs when the receptive person looks ahead and realizes they *will* want it. As one woman put it, "I will engage in sex for my husband's sake, knowing I will get in the mood eventually. Then things are usually great!"

This pattern is nearly twice as common among women (73 percent) as men (38 percent). But as you can see, with one in four women reporting initiating desire and more than one in three men reporting that their pattern is typically receptive, the gender patterns aren't universal.

If we don't recognize these two types of desire exist, one or both partners might think that the person with receptive desire needs to change to be healthy, sexually. That their desire

When does the feeling of desire arrive?

Different people may experience sexual desire / being "in the mood" at different stages of the process. Which statement is more true of you? (Choose One Answer)	Men	Women
Pattern characteristic of Initiating Desire	59%	24%
I tend to be in the mood for sex and want to pursue it with my spouse.		
Patterns characteristic of Receptive Desire	38%	73%
If my spouse initiates or mentions sex, or if something happens to make me think about sex (like a scene in a movie), that is when I am in the mood for it	13%	16%
If my spouse initiates sex, I am willing to get in the mood – and eventually will be in the mood once we get going	18%	36%
If my spouse initiates sex, I am willing to try – but I still may not end up in the mood. (Even if we keep going for my spouse's sake)	6%	21%
Pattern characteristic of being Resistant	4%	3%
If my spouse initiates sex, I'm really not that willing to try		

Source: MPS, n=916
Due to rounding, percentage totals for men slightly exceed 100% and total percent for receptive men (38%) slightly exceeds the subtotals shown for that category.

is "too low"—when, in fact, the *level* of desire is a completely different topic (which we'll tackle in the next chapter).

If we are wired differently, the goal isn't to make everyone the same or fit us into a mold of how things are "supposed" to be. The goal is to work with the type of desire we each have to come together well, for the health of our intimate life and the marriage.

FACT #3: We take on different desire "roles"

The fact that we *feel* desire in a different order isn't the end of the story. We may also *handle* things differently. And here is where some important nuance comes in. For some couples, initiating and receptive *actions* precisely follow the *feeling* of desire—for example, you feel desire, and you pursue your spouse (which is the case for 54 percent of men and just 16 percent of women.) Or, you haven't thought about sex all day, but your spouse gets frisky and you begin to respond.

But sometimes feelings and actions diverge. For example, you feel desire, but you take on the receptive role and wait for your spouse to initiate because you don't want to be pushy (which is the case for 27 percent of men and 24 percent of women). Or you *don't* feel desire, but you initiate with your spouse because it's been a few days and you know it's important for your marriage. I (Michael) call that "intentional desire," and it is an important pattern of action for many.

Talking about your pattern and your spouse's is a crucial step so you know what is going on in each other's mind and what you each are aiming for—or waiting for!

In an interview with me (Shaunti) and Jeff, one thirty-year-old couple with young children and two different desire types (he had initiating desire, she was receptive) described a relatively common dynamic.

DESIRE TYPES

HER: I'm usually pretty tired, and my husband is so sensitive to that. Almost *too* sensitive, actually! He doesn't want to be pushy.

HIM: Even though I'm usually in the mood, I want to be sure she *wants* it also. I know this is a hard season for her, with the kids. I would like sex every other day, but I know that is probably a bridge too far.

HER: But I want it too, you know. So if we're going to have sex, I usually initiate; it's the only way I can show him that I mean it!

HIM: Wait, what? That's what you're doing? How often do you actually *want* it?

HER: Like, every other day. Or almost that.

HIM: Really? Even now? (Laughing) I'm just realizing I shouldn't hold back so much!

HER: (Laughing) I feel like we've just had a counseling session, not an interview!

FACT #4: Anticipation time can "wake up" a receptive partner

For most couples with an initiating-receptive mismatch, one very encouraging reality is that receptive desire can be stimulated by the anticipation of sex—thinking about it ahead of time.

We've heard many of those who lean toward receptive desire say that throughout the day, sex simply doesn't occur to them; they just aren't as likely to be thinking about it. But if their spouse flirts with them beforehand, or does something to create anticipation, the receptive person may indeed start thinking about it! ("Wow, what a cold day! But maybe tonight we can, um, warm each other up.") That fun prompt—whatever works for that particular couple—helps the receptive spouse to look forward to what is to come and get their brain in gear *before* they get to the bedroom.

> A fun prompt helps the receptive spouse to think about sex *before* they get to the bedroom.

One happy couple Jeff and I (Shaunti) interviewed had started off rocky but within a few years had created a great intimate life. As the husband put it,

I've gotten it into my thick head that we're not the same. Initiating can be tricky. With two toddlers, at least one of us is tired. And I avoid initiating if there's a chance of getting the answer "I'm not feeling it tonight," because it hits me like rejection. But lately I've been trying to work *with* the differences instead of taking it personally. She has told me, "It's nice if you lay the groundwork." Which to her means I need to drop some hints. Do some touching that isn't provocative but closer to it. Like, she loves this little game where I try to secretly get a touch in on her boob when someone isn't looking. She says those are things that get her thinking about responding later, after we get the weasels to bed.

Another way to nurture anticipation time is with the intentional desire mentioned earlier. Just as most of us must be intentional to eat healthy, being intentional about sex is sometimes necessary too. It can provide the energy to spark arousal.

One great option is to schedule sex. While you can schedule initiation yourself, it is most effective when scheduled as a couple. Having it on the calendar doesn't simply set aside time in your busy schedules, it also provides that sense of anticipation for a receptive-desire partner.

It is crucial to note that anticipation time only works in the absence of negative responses by either spouse (like pressure, guilt, shame, sulking, or blaming). It is important that the initiating spouse remain loving and respectful and the receptive spouse open and receptive, anticipating how good it could be. It is also important to note that when sex is seen negatively (e.g., when there has been sexual trauma), this anticipation technique can be counterproductive and should be avoided.

In general, as long as the relationship is in a good place and they are open to it, giving a receptive-desire spouse some anticipation time—in whatever way *they* need—can dramatically change the overall outcome.

> **FACT #5:** How we handle a mismatch is more important than the physiological difference

The differences between us don't need to be obstacles; they can be wonderful opportunities to understand one another and deepen *marital*—not just sexual—intimacy in a profound way. Thus, how we *handle* an initiating-receptive mismatch has far more impact than solving the mismatch itself.

Tips for the initiator

Too often, a spouse with initiating desire misunderstands their partner's receptive desire. This can cause a domino effect of problems.

For example, it is common for a husband to feel rejected and vulnerable when he approaches his wife and sees her initial hesitation. She may have simply not been thinking about sex at all (if her default is neutral) and is now pondering whether she can hop straight into bed or whether she has to finish that accounting report for her boss first.

The husband's sense that she is *not* feeling the same desire for him can be painful in a foundational way (as you will see in chapter 6). He's assuming he is less desirable than an hour in front of the accounting analysis, when in fact, he *is* desirable to her, but in a completely different way.

If he responds negatively, it can be destructive to their sex life, thus pushing even receptive desire out of the picture. For example, I (Michael) have many times heard a wife describe her husband pouting, getting angry, distancing, or something similar. Which is *not* sexy or appealing![5] She may actually have been interested in having sex originally, but now she looks over and thinks, *But not with that.*

I encourage initiating-desire spouses to accept a "no" graciously and continue to foster a healthy setting for sex (more on this in chapter 8). I also suggest they view hesitancy as "Challenge accepted." In a marriage of goodwill, it makes a world of difference if a caring spouse sees hesitation as an opportunity to seduce their partner out of neutral and into drive over time. This seduction doesn't mean adopting a silent film–worthy pose and twirling a moustache. And it certainly doesn't mean pushing a spouse past their boundaries. What it does mean (as we will discuss later) is learning what is appealing to *your spouse*—and living that way. Both in the moment and at other times.

For example, a husband may keep his eyes open for a few weeks and realize that his wife first says, "No, I've got too much to do on the accounting report," but if he cheerfully says, "Another night then," and keeps being affectionate with her, she sometimes hops in the shower with him the next morning. Or an initiating-desire wife might observe her receptive-desire husband and learn what woos him out of work mode or house fix-it mode so he can consider sex as an option.

And conversely, the spouse who is saying no is encouraged to recognize when their spouse's "pouting" is actually because a painful insecurity has been triggered. Then they can look for ways to help their spouse manage their trigger, even if having sex isn't possible in that moment.

There is no magic formula. As we have said, the key is to lean in and learn your spouse.

Tips for the receptive spouse

As long as theirs is a marriage of goodwill, we encourage the receptive person to lean in as well. That may mean something tactical to get themselves thinking about sex, like setting a reminder to initiate once in a while and enjoy their spouse's reaction! Or focusing on their spouse's emotional desire to connect intimately with them.

This is especially important when a marriage season is challenging and the receptive spouse wants to ensure their intimate relationship doesn't suffer. If the receptive spouse focuses on the pressure, duty, responsibility, or cost of not engaging, they are getting caught in the mire. Instead, we invite them to look for what they can appreciate in their spouse, allow that to seduce and soften them, and choose to engage, knowing it will be good for them in a few minutes and they'll be glad they did. (If it *isn't* usually good, or if receptive desire doesn't kick in, it means something else is likely going on in the marriage that needs to be attended to.)

Use Wiring Differences to Create a Dynamic Love Life

As you consider these overall suggestions, think about how to apply them to *your* individual situation. We have posted several application resources at our website.

- *Be curious.* Always start with curiosity. Curiosity is incompatible with contempt, criticism, blame, and a host of other destructive stances—especially when talking about sex with your spouse.

- *Accept that your spouse's sexual desire is different, not deficient.* If you subconsciously continue to believe something is *wrong* with your spouse for being different than what you expect, it will be difficult for you to come together well.

You might wonder, *But what if something is wrong? What if my spouse does indeed have a physical or mental problem? What if my spouse is resistant?* As you know, there are a host of specialized situations we can't cover here. But solutions do exist. Please seek a trained and experienced sex therapy/ sexual medicine professional to help you. (See our website for a list of specialists.)

- *Similarly, accept that you are not broken.* Whether you are a receptive- or initiating-desire person, recognize that your type of desire is the way you are. You're not a sex maniac just because you think about sex more, and you're not frigid just because you don't. Honor your design as you connect sexually with your spouse in a way that is authentic for you.

- *Ask your spouse about their desire type and desire role.* As a starting point, we suggest each of you circle your individual type of desire on the grid on the next page. Then find the square where you and your spouse intersect. (The number represents what percent of couples have that pattern.) Then see the next steps, below.

- *Brainstorm solutions.* Next, looking at where each of you fall on the grid, consider what might help you work with your types of desire and what solutions would help both of you.

What are the desire types of each member of a couple?

		Wives		
		Initiating 16.2%	Receptive 75.5%	Resistant 8.3%
Husbands	Initiating 53.9%	5.2%	43.0%	5.7%
	Receptive 41.0%	9.6%	29.3%	2.2%
	Resistant 5.09%	1.3%	3.3%	0.4%

Source: MPS, n=916, heterosexual couples only.
Husbands' totals do not equal 100% due to rounding.

In only 5% of couples do *both* partners have initiating desire.

Let's consider a hypothetical example. Suppose you wish there was more sex happening. But you are also receptive rather than initiating. If your spouse is also receptive, however, you now realize they probably *aren't* going to initiate in the way you would love. Since you're the one who wants more, you also realize that probably won't happen unless *you* initiate or both of you come up with another solution.

The key is to stop being on opposite sides of the table to negotiate who does what and how often, and instead put yourself on the same side of the table and figure out creative solutions *together*. (For example, scheduling sex.)

- *Establish an intentional, healthy pattern.* If you are initiating, *choose* to live in a way that draws your spouse in, inside and outside the bedroom, flirt with them (if that is what your spouse wants), and be gracious when their car just isn't going to be in drive that day. If you are receptive, *choose* to engage with your spouse sexually, and keep a positive cycle going. For example, keep sex in mind and try initiating. If your physiology makes it likely that you simply *won't* be in the mood as often as is needed to create a thriving intimate life with your spouse, consider making the choice to engage while knowing the feelings will catch up.

When Desire Differences Become an Opportunity

Our differences around desire don't have to pull us apart. They can present an opportunity for us to be curious and actively learn each other. To grow. To practice thoughtfulness. To own what is needed on our end without making our actions conditional on what our spouse does ("I'll do X once he/she does Y"). And ultimately, to build a focus on our spouse and not ourselves—which will transform everything in marriage.

As I (Shaunti) was sharing with a friend what I had learned on this topic, she made a wise point:

> I think on this topic we have to realize: "I'm never *not* going to have to work on this thing." The person who doesn't think about making love as much may not be naturally drawn toward that thought—but they need to *do* things that make sex come up in their mind. And the person who does think about sex may not be naturally drawn toward the attention that is needed to their spouse outside the bedroom—and they may need to purposefully work every day on things like affirming their spouse, listening, speaking their partner's love language. We need to simply *expect* that we will always need to work on this.

In the end, being purposeful about things we *want* to do but that may not come naturally allows us to be ourselves . . . while still honoring our differences. Which, if you think about it, is one of the great things about the two becoming one.

DESIRE TYPES

5

"i want you to want me"

*how purposeful connection is even
more important than desire levels*

THE SURPRISE: Even with desire differences, we are not as far apart in what we want as it might seem—which makes bridging the gap easier than we might think.

When you get married, how much sex do you want?"

The man Jeff was interviewing had nervously asked his girlfriend this question before the two of them were engaged. Both were in their late twenties and both had had sexual relationships with other partners. Yet as their faith had become more important, they had determined they would wait until marriage.

But the man wanted to know what he would be getting into. As he told Jeff, "I would love my wife to be a godly, kind woman who is the picture of respect in the community. *But when I get her home . . .*" He grinned and let his thought trail off. "Since I'm not going to find that out *before* our wedding night, I sort of figured we had to have that conversation."

He was delighted (and relieved) that his girlfriend was looking for active, adventurous sexual engagement after marriage too. This man thought he needed to ask this question to be sure she wanted "enough." But when they talked, they discovered that her desire level was quite a bit higher than his. (He was thinking twice a week; she was an almost-every-day sort of person.) He originally thought this was every young man's dream, but quickly realized it could cause problems if she felt deprived because he wasn't in the mood as often.

But as they discussed it, they realized what they both cared about most was their expectations for the quality and type of sexual connection. They wanted to know their eventual spouse was willing to be open and adventurous in bed (or out of it!). When they focused on that, rather than on the fact that she wanted twice as much sex as he did, their worries smoothed out.

Desire Levels Aren't the Only—Or Even the Main—Factor

It is easy to think the main thing that matters for regular sexual connection is how often each partner wants sex. When you're not connecting as much as you want, it is easy to focus on your different levels of desire.

Yet in most marriages, *we don't actually need to increase or decrease one person's desire* in the way we assume . . . because we are not nearly as far apart as we think we are.

Not long ago, I (Shaunti) was talking with a pastor about Jeff and me coming to speak at his church's annual marriage event. He asked if one of our sessions could be on intimacy, explaining, "In counseling, we've noticed that although some men and women do have wildly different desire levels, most are fairly close. It just doesn't *seem* like it because it is activated so differently. Once they realize that, they stop thinking, 'Well, my partner just doesn't want it as much' and instead start thinking it is totally *feasible* to connect—which then allows them to figure it out!"

Connection and Application Points

Rather than wishing we or our partner could change, imagine if we could focus on how to take our individual desire types (covered in the last chapter) and desire levels (covered

DESIRE LEVELS

in this chapter) and figure out how to turn that into a recipe to connect in our marriage in a way that works for us.

As with other concepts in this book, this chapter includes generalizations about common patterns among men and women. But if you don't align with patterns common to your sex, remember chapter 2: You are normal.*

Also, be aware that sexual desire is incredibly complex. It is a mix of intricate biology (multiple chemicals and systems), emotion, meaning, relationship, culture, and value. The solution is never as simple as "take this pill." And our generalizations are helpful, but they are still generalizations. Your sexual desire may be different than what you or your spouse think it should be.

Thankfully, if we keep a few points in mind, most spouses can work to discover each other and connect well.

> **POINT #1:** Conflict or distress around sexual desire is normal in marriage

We have a word for couples who have conflict about sexual desire—whether it is frequency or what and how they do it. That word is *normal*.

---

*Because this chapter is fundamentally about male-female relationships, and because those in same-sex marriages tended toward substantially different desire patterns (which can only be understood through additional research), most of the data in this chapter is from mixed-sex couples only. (MPS unless otherwise noted.)

If you're having tension around sex in your marriage—getting into arguments or feeling disappointed, stressed, or hurt—you are in good company. Sex is one of the primary causes of arguments in marriage, and the top sex-related concern is the simple pain of wanting something different than what is happening—especially a different *amount* of sex.

Now, some couples—21 percent!—are happily on the same page about how often they want sex.[1] But the vast majority—79 percent—are not. And that disconnect can result in a high level of pain. In fact, in the study of married couples I (Michael) conducted for my doctoral dissertation, the pain was so great, more than *half of the couples had considered or sought professional help* for issues around desire.[2]

DESIRE LEVELS

Do couples want the same frequency of sex?

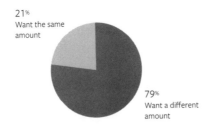

21% Want the same amount

79% Want a different amount

Source: MPS, n=458 couples. Heterosexual couples only.

As we'll discuss in the next chapter, sexual issues feed our swirling insecurities and worries and can create other issues that exacerbate the sexual disconnect. This happens even within the most well-meaning of couples in great marriages.

Thankfully, this common pattern doesn't have to be the end of the story.

POINT #2: A different level of desire doesn't mean a lack of desire

Remember the car analogy from the last chapter? If the *type* of desire that you feel can be compared to a car being in drive, neutral, or reverse, the *level* of desire you feel can be compared to the level of fuel in the car.[3] Sometimes, when we don't see one partner "moving," the issue is that they are in neutral instead of drive. They have plenty of fuel, it just hasn't been activated yet.

But sometimes we do indeed have two different levels of fuel in our tanks. Let's take a quick look at what we found about the differences between us. (See chart on next page.) As noted, in 79 percent of couples the spouses have different levels of desire. The husband has the higher desire in 54 percent of marriages, and the wife has the higher desire in 24 percent of marriages.[4] (Due to rounding, those percentages don't quite total 79 percent.)

Note that while men are more than twice as likely as women to have the higher desire, in one in four marriages, it is the *wife* who wants more sex than her husband.[5]

Who has the highest desire in Married Couples?

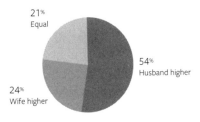

21% Equal

54% Husband higher

24% Wife higher

Source: MPS, n=458 couples.
Calculated desire for heterosexual couples only. Totals do not equal 100% due to rounding.

I (Shaunti) have talked to so many women at my events who see themselves as weird or abnormal because (as one put it), "What we hear at marriage conferences is that the husband is the one chasing his wife around the bed. But in my relationship, *I'm* the one chasing my husband around the bed!"

If that is you, you clearly are not alone. And application tools and advice for higher-desire spouses will generally help, regardless of gender.

The key point here is this: Our tanks may indeed be at different levels. Yet unless it runs out entirely, each car does have fuel! In the vast majority of cases, there is still a way both cars can go on regular drives together and be happy about the process. It may be as simple as getting creative and figuring out how to create a regular pattern that *works* for both.

DESIRE LEVELS

POINT #3: We are not as far apart as we think

The very good news is that, usually, two different partners ultimately want the same thing. We both want connection, we both want pleasure, we both want intimacy, and we often even want all that in roughly similar frequency—but we approach it differently. We may each need something different to keep our "fuel levels" up. Or we might want to use our fuel completely differently: One person may want a leisurely drive, while the other wants a high-speed chase.

> We both want connection and pleasure, and often in roughly similar frequency— but we approach it differently.

Often, those differences are getting in the way, rather than a truly large difference in desire level or a lack of interest. It is crucial to grasp this, since the incorrect *belief* that we are far apart in desire levels can cause way more distress than the actual differences. Which, often, are not as wide as we think.

Take the graph of how much sex husbands and wives said they wanted. Notice anything? The desired amount is *extraordinarily* similar, overall. Yes, there are some differences within individual couples, but in general, not nearly as many as popularly assumed. Only 30 percent of couples have a substantial mismatch on how much sex each partner wants.[6]

How often would you like sex?

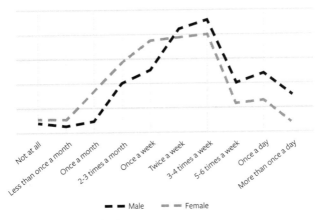

Source: MPS n=916, heterosexuals only

A common interchange when I (Michael) counsel couples who have tension over sexual frequency goes like this:

ME: How often do each of you want sex?

HER: I don't know . . . maybe one to two times a week?

HIM: About two to three times a week.

ME: There's not much difference between two and two.

Some couples, of course, will be much further apart. Yet even then, if the relationship were healthier or if other issues were addressed, their ideals might be closer. Especially because the vast majority of lower-desire spouses wish they were wired differently. As one representative woman put it, "I don't believe my lower sex drive is fair to my husband. I want to want it, but I'm not sure how to get there."

Another woman asked, "What is the best way to overcome the exhaustion of working full time and having two toddlers? I just don't want sex at all, but I do want the intimacy." The truth is that this wife clearly *does* want sex—she just doesn't *think* of it as wanting sex. Which means that if she and/or her husband can come up with creative solutions (including everything from his taking more toddler duty to some of the ideas for stimulating desire, below) they may be able to connect more often.

> **POINT #4:** In many cases, both spouses want more sex than they are getting

Very often, the issue *isn't* that one person is getting less sex than they want: It is that *both* people are getting less sex than they want! Take the next graph, which charts how much sex both partners *want* (which you saw above) and how much they are actually *getting*.

Notice anything? It turns out, in most cases, *neither* spouse is getting as much sex as they would like![7]

How often would you like sex versus how often is it happening?

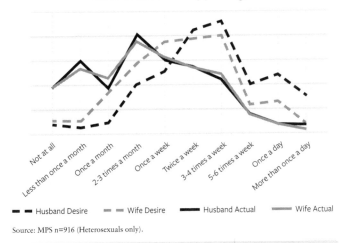

Husband Desire   Wife Desire   Husband Actual   Wife Actual

Source: MPS n=916 (Heterosexuals only).

Both men and women want more sex than they are getting.

When we are dissatisfied with the amount of sex we are getting, it is very easy to think, as we pout in the corner, that our spouse is completely fine with it. Yet that's probably not true! Among those who said they were less than happy with the frequency, 76 percent of their spouses were less than happy with the frequency too![8] Even in most low-sex/no-sex marriages, *both* the husband and wife want to be having sex more often!

When neither spouse is getting as much sex as they would like, it completely changes the dynamic. Instead of feeling like we have to fix one or both of the *people*, we can instead try to figure out the *problem* that's getting in the way. Instead of the higher-desire person asking, "Why aren't *you* having sex?" we both need to ask, "Why aren't *we* having sex?"

> Instead of the higher-desire person asking, "Why aren't *you* having sex?" we both need to ask, "Why aren't *we* having sex?"

For example, is one partner always up late cleaning the kitchen and the other falls asleep before the tidy partner makes it to bed? Perhaps we work out a shared solution for cleaning the kitchen so *both* partners go to bed at the same time. Or are both spouses a bit cranky from work all day and simply not in a good relational place to be intimate at night? Perhaps the solution is a morning date in the shower when getting ready for work, twice a week.

I (Michael) can tell you, after many years in my clinical practice: Solutions exist. Recognizing that we are more similar than we realize allows us to stop being adversarial. We can instead put ourselves on the same team to solve a *joint* problem and reduce distress.

> **POINT #5:** Overall, higher-desire spouses are more distressed than their lower-desire or equal-desire counterparts

As we analyzed the data, we saw a consistent pattern. First, there is a statistically significant relationship between how often someone wants sex, compared with how often their spouse wants it, and the level of satisfaction (or dissatisfaction) they tend to experience in the sexual relationship. Those with the most tension and disappointment tended to be the spouse with a higher desire than their mate.[9]

Conversely, those with the least conflict and the most satisfaction appeared to be those with a desire equal to that of their spouse. Those with a lower desire than their spouse were somewhere in the middle.

Which makes sense. The higher-desire spouse probably has the greatest gap between what they want and what is happening. As one woman put it, "My sex drive seems to be stronger than his and it is not fun to always feel like you are begging for sex, especially being the woman."

Of course, there are many exceptions to these patterns. But out of love and care for our spouse—especially if we are married to a higher-desire spouse—it is important to be able to see how our individual patterns are impacting them.

DESIRE LEVELS

> **POINT #6:** The lower-desire spouse tends to control how often sex is happening—and can use that for good or for ill

The lower-desire spouse tends to be the one who has control over the tempo of the sexual relationship. As one higher-desire husband explained, "Although I am the higher-desire partner and attempt to initiate conversations and actions that lead to intimacy, my wife is the one who ultimately decides when it will happen. So even though I would say I initiate, I am actually waiting on the green light from her before the next step can be taken."

Or, as a higher-desire wife put it, "I would like sex more often, but I have to wait until he wants it."

The lower-desire spouse rarely thinks of themselves as holding the power in their sex life. And yet the high-desire spouse tends to want more power—they wish they had a way to make it happen more often. This unintentional power struggle can tear at the foundation of marriage.

So let's speak directly to the lower-desire spouses for a moment. Rather than feeling powerless, realize: *Wait a minute. I actually hold much of the power in our sex life.* In my (Michael's) clinical practice, I have seen that once a lower-desire spouse realizes their power and leans in, their marriage has the potential to become particularly playful and rich.

As one example, imagine a marriage where the husband is higher desire. If he approaches his wife and she embraces the opportunity she holds, she can make it a sensual time or a playful time by how she says yes. He can't make it playful if she's not open to it. He can't make it erotic if she's not open to it. But she can, by how she responds. It works the same if we flip genders. In couples where the husband is the low-desire spouse, this pattern is often even more powerful.

Yet there is equal responsibility for the higher-desire spouse. They must live in a way that is appealing to their spouse rather than demanding their way. Overpowering a spouse's no in any way is not reflective of Christ and is always abusive and wrong.[10]

> **POINT #7:** The fact that your spouse has lower desire doesn't mean you aren't desirable

When we aren't pursued, it's easy to believe we aren't desirable. As one higher-desire woman asked, "Is there a way to feel pursued, when my husband is 'receptive' and not a pursuer? I wonder about how desirable I am when I am not pursued."

The main answer is that we have to be willing to tell ourselves the truth. Because while there may indeed be cases in which our spouse doesn't find us attractive, most of the time, a spouse doesn't pursue *because they aren't wired to*. If your

DESIRE LEVELS

spouse says they find you desirable, accept it. Don't use their desire intensity or activity as the measure of your desirability.

> **POINT #8:** We may deeply long for sex but we don't "need" sex

This whole book emphasizes the deep importance of sex for us and our marriages. But a common message in culture and Christian circles pushes past "importance" and calls sex a "need." I (Michael) believe we must shift away from that teaching.

Our true needs as humans are minimal. Without the basic physical needs of food and water, we die. Without the basic emotional need of human connection, we experience real suffering and failure to thrive. Sex is not in that same category. Research has tried and failed to prove from multiple angles that sex is a need. Additionally, many people live full lives without sex—because they have a significantly disabled spouse, are asexual, feel called to be single and celibate, or for other reasons (even if some may still long for things to be otherwise).

When we assert that sex is a need, it implies that we have to have sex. Not true. It is a God-designed drive we are called to discipline for good.[11] We are not enslaved to that part of our nature.

Further, terming sex a need also implies that our spouse must "meet our need," and turn sex into their "duty" no matter how they feel or what is going on in the relationship.

("I need this, and you are the only person I can get it from.") These perspectives are dishonoring and destructive to both men and women and to the core of marriage.

Once we recognize sex as richer than a need, we can put sexual connection into the beautiful context in which it belongs. Sex is freed to be about discipline and desire, not just duty and drive. We are freed to truly *choose* to initiate and receive as a way to serve and love one another well.

> **POINT #9:** Withholding sex because it "isn't a need" is incompatible with a loving relationship

Just because we can't claim sex as a need doesn't mean it loses any importance. Sexual intimacy is a critical part of the marital covenant and of a God-reflective marriage. Choosing *not* to make sex a priority is no more acceptable than demanding it.

We seek to honor what is good for the marriage and pleases each of us. We may not think of it this way, but when we choose to *not* work on sexual intimacy, we put unhealthy selfish desires ahead of the good of our marriage and our spouse—which will always be destructive.

There may be an understandable reason for not being very sexual (e.g., a physical issue or healing from trauma). But as noted earlier, we can almost always engage in some form of sexual activity.

POINT #10: Desire isn't a static thing

Finally, and hopefully most encouraging: Desire isn't fixed. We have physiological tendencies, but our physiology changes over time. Childbirth, a new job, new seasons of life, disease, medications, trauma, and aging all change our bodies and typically negatively impact desire. Sleep, exercise, sunlight, and healthy diet are physical changes that can positively impact desire.

We also have choices. And sometimes those choices alter our physiology—or even our spouse's!—around desire.

Sexual activity stimulates sexual desire.

Consistent with Newton's first law of motion, couples who have a regular pattern of sexual activity tend to keep a consistent pattern well into old age. This could be due to a number of factors (including habit), but part of it is likely body related. A lot of chemicals are released during healthy sex that foster a desire for sex. For example, being regularly sexually stimulated by sexual activity or anticipation of sexual activity *actually results in raised levels of testosterone—which is one of the chemicals facilitating desire for many.* Conversely, forgoing sex can cause testosterone levels to drop.[12]

Thus, not having sex may become a vicious cycle. You have less sex, so sexual chemical levels drop, and you want even less sex. Which makes it even more likely you'll forgo sex . . . and so on.

But, encouragingly, choosing to have sex can create a positive cycle and even become self-sustaining. As long as you're in a reasonably healthy situation, when you "go for it" and *decide* to regularly engage with your spouse, your sexual chemistry will be stimulated and you will likely begin to want sex more. Which means you'll have sex more often, which means you'll continue to produce those chemicals that keep you more open to sex.

Therefore, one principle that often works is: *If you want to want sex, have sex.*

One principle that often works is: *If you want to want sex, have sex.*

Of course, this is not a magic-wand solution; for many couples, addressing interpersonal dynamics is more important. And there will be occasions and relationships where the "have sex to want sex" pattern would not be healthy—or even possible. But overall, it is a helpful principle.

A partner's attention and care can drastically change the desire dynamic.

For many lower-desire spouses, their desire profile often hinges on their view of how affirming and caring their partner is—or is not. One man in a difficult marriage (and with an anemic love life) told Jeff, "My wife is so critical. She says I don't do enough around the house—but when I try, I don't do it right. She always mentions it when I burn the dinner or forget something on the list at the grocery store. It is as if she is constantly emasculating me—and then wanting me to make love to her that night. It does *not* work that way. In order to want to be with her, I need to hear her say 'good job' once in a while, and mean it."

When a partner wakes up to the need to attend to their spouse outside the bedroom—which should be the norm in a healthy marriage anyway!—it can often lead to more interest inside the bedroom. In other words—it is as if they are regularly putting more fuel in their spouse's tank.

In the research with women that Jeff and I (Shaunti) did for *For Men Only*, nearly three out of four women (73 percent) said they would want to make love more frequently if their husband would maintain or increase his level of emotional attention to them. (See chart on next page.) We suspect that attention and verbal affirmation from higher-desire wives may result in a similar response from lower-desire husbands.

We love what one woman wrote in: "When it comes to sex, I am naturally a Crock-Pot and my husband is a microwave. But he does a wonderful job of what we call keeping me 'microwaveable': He is very attentive almost 24/7. It's important to us to keep each other interested and to *know*

	Not particularly helpful	Very helpful	Total
Are there more things that your husband can do to increase the chances that you will want to make love more frequently? Please rate the helpfulness of each of the following statements.			
Maintain or increase his level of emotional attention to me	27%	73%	100%
Create a context where he often shows me little gestures of love throughout the day	29%	71%	100%
Engage in caring, listening, and conversation regularly	33%	67%	100%

Source: *For Men Only*

DESIRE LEVELS

that we are loved and desired. It's been twenty-one years and going strong."

Now, *how* you show attention and affirmation to fill your partner's tank will vary—because what matters to your spouse will vary. One male client told me (Michael), "I found out what turns my wife on: tea."

"What kind?" I asked, thinking I needed to buy some stock.

"The kind doesn't matter," he said. "I fix her a cup of tea and sit across from her and explore how she is *really* doing. I spend some time being her 'girlfriend,' really listening to her."

His wife chimed in, "After he has spent time being really focused on me and listening to me, I'm grabbing him by the collar and saying, 'Come on, big boy, I'm eager to do more than talk.'"

As you consider how to fill your partner's tank, keep in mind that there is no formula. At least not one *we* can give you. The example above might not be at all what works for your spouse—or for you. As Jeff put it, "For some men, the idea of talking over tea will feel way too awkward. But maybe he can talk while they are cooking dinner, or while working side by side on the yard. Whether it is the husband or wife, the template isn't any one action. The template is finding what helps one spouse feel connected to the other spouse. And the best way to find that out is to ask."

Simple Steps That Will Help

The encouragement of this "we are closer than we think" truth is that in most cases, simple steps really will make a difference. We suggest starting with these four.

- *Get curious and ask each other the basics.* Assume you don't know what your spouse will say. How often do each of you *want* sex? How often is it actually happening? How does your *type* of desire impact you?

We recommend that you take our simple, free assessment via our website. But as a starting point, now that you understand both desire types and desire levels, enter and discuss where each of you individually falls on this next grid.

	Is your desire typically higher, the same, or lower than your spouse?		
		I have higher desire	We are the same	I have lower desire
Which desire type are you most often like?	Initiating			
	Receptive			
	Resistant			

DESIRE LEVELS

- *Ask each other "What matters?" and "What can I do?"* Discuss what would most fill your tank, and your partner's. Do you feel capable of doing the action that would fill your spouse's tank? If not, what would be feasible?

- *Identify the issues that might be getting in the way and discuss solutions.* Do you both want more sex? If so, figure out the *joint* problem keeping you both from what you want, and tackle it together.

  It may mean adjusting or compromising on things you wouldn't have imagined before. ("What do you mean I can clean the kitchen in the morning instead of after the kids are in bed?!") It may mean working on something that is getting in the way, like getting therapy to deal with past sexual abuse or a hair-trigger temper. No matter what, always keep the greater good—your marriage, and the intimate oil for your marital engine—in mind.

Explore your "self-sustaining" frequency. If you are the lower-desire partner, explore whether there is a threshold frequency of sex that stimulates you to *want* sex more. Experiment with what threshold works for *both* of you. Assuming you have a sexually safe marriage, try forty days of a chosen pattern (for example, weekly, every other day, or twice a week) and see if you find one that works for the two of you. For multiple reasons, I (Michael) encourage most couples to try to keep their engagement at once a week or more.

Give Grace in the Differences

Despite our best efforts, there may be some seasons we simply won't be able to have sex as often as one or both spouses would like. It could be because of young kids. Or a third-shift job. Or a taxing travel schedule. There may also be some ways in which we realize we will always be different. But because we are now on the same team, we will be realizing that *together*. And we can give one another grace in those differences.

As we were finishing the book, one husband sent us this email. He had been using some of our advance research to try to truly understand his wife of thirty years—and learned more than he'd ever expected:

Over the years, I had been a bit sad that my wife didn't seem to *want* me in a sexual way—or at least not the way I wanted her. There has been some grief associated with that. Dissatisfaction. But these last few months, as I've been talking to her and trying to understand how she *actually* works, that dissatisfaction has been replaced with pure admiration and love.

All this time, my wife has been working to connect with me in the intimate ways I wanted—but I wasn't seeing it correctly. A higher-desire person thinks their spouse is sexually engaging because they are attracted to them or wanting sexual satisfaction in the same way. But I finally realized: My spouse is *choosing* me. She doesn't feel the physical urge as strongly as I do, and she is choosing me anyway! That is radical. It makes me feel loved and desired—even though the desire is different from what I thought I wanted. It makes me so thankful for her.

I hope *all* higher-desire people can understand this and give their spouse the credit they deserve. Because that will transform how we see each other.

6

sexual healing

*what sex—and the process
of getting there—says to our hearts*

THE SURPRISE: Men and women tend to have different insecurities that the process of sex can help heal or hurt.

On October 9, 2021, a twenty-one-year-old Texas A&M football player named Seth Small created the upset of the last twenty years by kicking a dramatic last-play-of-the-game field goal to beat perennial powerhouse Alabama, which had not lost to an unranked team in fourteen years.

A viral video captured the dramatic reactions of his wife and family.[1] Seth's mom can't watch and appears to be praying. His newlywed wife hoarsely cheers him on, tensely watches, anxiously tracks the trajectory of his kick with her eyes . . . and breaks down in sobs. Then she jumps up, hurdles the wall, and races out onto the field to find him.

This type of "give you the feels" video (as several sports articles put it) often goes viral because it is shared by vast networks of women. But in this case, hardened male sports-writers and sports-watchers were also sharing a video clip that was not of the actual game-winning kick—and trying to explain why it impacted them so much.

One man who sent it to me (Shaunti) said, "This is what every man wants—especially the end!"

I emailed back, "You mean when the wife jumps the wall? Or just her tears?"

He replied, "All of it. It sounds so cheesy, but it feels like, 'You're my hero.' More than that, he IS a hero. That's what every man wants to be but doubts he can be."

There is a really important truth hidden in these reactions, but before we explain, let's flip to a different short video segment that elicits a surprising emotional reaction from many women.

In the live-action 2015 *Cinderella* movie, there's a moment when the prince has almost overcome Cinderella's reluctance to share her name. Suddenly, the clock starts to chime midnight. Anxious about the magic being broken, she jumps up and rushes away saying she is so sorry, she loved every moment, but she has to go![2]

The prince, clearly baffled, sits down slowly as she disappears. He quotes something curious that she said. And then he looks in the direction she ran and a grin spreads over his face. With a determined look, he jumps up and runs after her.[3]

And that is where many women have an unexpected reaction. One woman tried to explain it. "I'm a pretty strong person, so I'm embarrassed to admit this, but I literally catch my breath when I see that *look* on his face. That pursuit. That he found her so appealing that he wasn't going to let her get away. She ran—but it didn't matter. She was worth running after."

Two short video clips. Two sets of unexpected reactions. What, you might ask, does this have to do with sex?

Everything.

Deep Vulnerabilities

Sex has the ability to profoundly touch our hearts. This is in part because in the connection of sex, we are exposed. More specifically, our *insecurities* are exposed.

All of us have insecurities hidden deep inside—and the acute ones beg for comfort. When we hear, "This thing you're especially insecure about? You don't have to be. You're amazing," the emotional impact is profound.

The thing is, we don't always think about the fact that our spouse has deep insecurities too—or that they are likely different from ours. And if their acute insecurities are different, what will reassure and comfort them will be different. In other words: Our spouse probably doesn't just have different core *insecurities*, but different core emotional *needs*.

> Our spouse probably doesn't just have different core *insecurities*, but different core emotional *needs*.

In part, this happens because we are simply different people. But it also happens, as research continues to reveal, because the most intensely felt (or core) insecurities and needs tend to be different in men and women.

Here are two key implications. If our spouse has different core insecurities than we do, what wounds them will be very different than what wounds us. And if we have different emotional needs, then words or actions that would be life-giving to us will merely feel nice if directed toward our spouse.

Thankfully, there is great news: Once we understand these deep truths about our spouse, we have an excellent opportunity to build the intimacy we are longing for—because sex hits the deepest places of all.

Hidden Truths

The data in this chapter is drawn not only from new research for this book, but from multiple other studies that I (Shaunti) conducted for other books over the years—especially for *For Women Only: What You Need to Know about the Inner Lives of Men* and *For Men Only: A Straightforward Guide to the Inner Lives of Women.*[4]

For simplicity's sake we'll be painting with a broad brush and saying, "men tended to say X" and "women tended to think Z," even though quite a few people (roughly 20 to 30 percent, depending on the topic) have patterns more like their opposite-sex fellows.* Always keep in mind that what matters is what is true of you and your spouse, and use this as a starting point for conversation.

Let's jump in. You may think the first hidden truth below has nothing to do with sex. But you'll see that, just like the stories above, it really does.

> **TRUTH #1:** Men and women tend to report markedly different emotional factors under the surface

A number of years ago, I (Shaunti) conducted focus groups on back-to-back evenings; the first night for a group of young

---

*Because this chapter is specifically focused on male-female relationships, all the data in this chapter is from heterosexual marriages unless otherwise noted.

men, the next for young women—all in their early twenties. The first night, I opened up one of the whiteboards on the wall and asked the eight or so guys to determine the core insecurities and needs they had inside. What words or actions would most make them feel bad and what would light them up? They took the assignment seriously, and at the end of the night I closed the doors to hide the whiteboard.

The next night, I opened up the other whiteboard and asked the young women to determine the core insecurities and needs they had as women. One participant protested. "I object to this language. It's not our insecurities and our needs as *women*. We're all just people. We have the same feelings."

"Great," I said. "Let's chart your insecurities and needs as people."

We spent all evening on it, and once we were done, I asked if they wanted to see what the guys had said the night before. They were intrigued. But when I opened up both whiteboards, the room got very quiet. What they were seeing clearly rocked their previously held beliefs: *Not one word was the same.*

Across twenty years of research around the globe, it is clear that certain important emotional factors—the deepest fears and desires in our hearts—simply tend to be different between most men and most women. And they tend to impact many aspects of our lives, not just marriage and sex.

We can have great discussions on *why* this is, and whether or not it "should" be this way (discussions beyond the scope of this book), but the data shows these differences *exist*.

Here's an overall summary of what we (Jeff and Shaunti) have seen to be the case for roughly 70 to 80 percent of men and women, depending on the audience or research instrument.

Women

In general, the core insecurities for women—the most acute hidden worries or questions—are: "Am I loveable? Special? Beautiful? Am I worthy of being loved for who I am on the inside?"

And these questions aren't answered positively just because a woman gets married to a great guy or even has her picture on the cover of a magazine. They just morph into "Does he *really* love me?" "Does *he* think I'm beautiful?"

More than eight in ten women on the *For Men Only* survey indicated that they sometimes felt insecure about their man's love or the relationship. (See chart on next page.) And this wasn't a rare thing, or sparked only by conflict. Almost seven in ten women (68 percent) said those sorts of thoughts (such as wondering how their husband felt about them) were either occasionally or often in their mind. Less than one-third said those thoughts only came up during difficult relationship seasons or never at all.

INSECURITY

Do women ever feel insecure "about his love or the relationship?"	
At times feel insecure about his love or the relationship	82%
Never feel insecure about his love or the relationship	18%

Source: *For Men Only*

So let's pause with a question for men: How often do *you* worry about whether your wife loves you? Or how the relationship is going? Some of you (particularly in struggling marriages) will say those thoughts arise regularly. But most tell us they just don't come up. That's because you're not dealing with a deep "Am I loveable?" question in your heart.

Now, to be clear, this vulnerability doesn't mean your wife thinks you *don't* love her. But something inside her may always be subconsciously looking to you for signals about the answer to that question.

This is why most women feel an emotional need to feel loved and cherished. To feel beautiful and special. To feel pursued. Whatever makes her feel that way (which could be as simple as your texting "I love you" in the middle of her workday) isn't just nice but *powerful*, because it is speaking affirmation directly to the area of greatest insecurity.

And that is why the scene in *Cinderella* so unexpectedly touches the hearts of women who have long ago set aside fairy tales; it tugs at a deep longing to be someone who is worth going after—and who is special enough that her man takes *delight* in pursuing her.

Men

In general, the most acute insecurity and question in the heart of men is not "Am I loveable?" but "Am I *able*?" In other words, am I adequate? Do I have what it takes? Am I any good at what I *do*?

And these questions aren't resolved just because a man is a great dad or a famous CEO. They just morph into, "Does *she* believe I'm a great dad?" "Is she proud of me?" "Does she see what I've done and say it is good?"

Men tend to project an "I've got this covered" confidence, but privately tell us it is just a mask. Three out of four men (76 percent) on our workplace survey for *The Male Factor* said, "I am not always as confident as I look." That underground self-doubt is so painful that most men shy away from feeling it at all costs—especially with their wife. Three in four men on the *For Women Only* survey said that if they had to make a choice, feeling inadequate was far more painful than feeling unloved: If they had to, they would give up feeling their wife loved them if they could feel that she respected them! (See chart on next page.)

Women rightly point out, "I need respect too." Of course you do! But in focus groups and events with thousands of

Men: Think about what these two negative experiences would be like: to feel alone and unloved in the world OR to feel inadequate and disrespected by everyone. If you were forced to choose one, which would you prefer? Would you rather feel...? (Choose one answer.)	
Alone and Unloved	74%
Inadequate and Disrespected	26%

Source: *For Women Only*

women over the years, most women—if forced to choose—would not *give up* feeling loved to get respect and appreciation. Most men would.

So here's the question for the women reading this: How often do you worry about whether your husband thinks you are good at what you do? Whether he believes you're a good mom, for example, or whether he thinks you did a good enough job on that big project of painting the sunroom? Some of you (especially in a difficult marriage) will say those thoughts arise regularly. But most women tell us it just doesn't come up. That's because you're not dealing with an underground "Am I able/good at what I do?" question in your heart.

To be clear, this "Am I able?" vulnerability doesn't mean your husband thinks you find him incompetent! But something inside him may always be subconsciously looking to you for signals about the answer to that question.

This is why most men feel a powerful longing to be appreciated and respected. To feel admired and believed in. To hear, "That thing you just did (cleaning the kitchen, handling the kids' argument, getting that old lawnmower running) was good." Whatever makes him feel that way (which can be as simple as saying, "Thank you for cleaning up the kitchen") isn't just nice but *powerful*, because it is speaking affirmation directly to the area of greatest insecurity.

And that is why the video of Seth Small's wife rooting her husband on to do something incredible and leaping the wall to find him so unexpectedly touches the hearts of men: It tugs at a deep longing to be noticed for accomplishing something so good—and to have the most important person in his life be that proud of him.

It's not our responsibility—it's our opportunity.

We should be able to understand each other's most acute insecurities because most of us feel those insecurities and needs to some degree as well.

Now, just to be clear, it is *not* our responsibility to make our spouse feel good about themselves, or their responsibility to do the same for us. We are each responsible for our own view of self—ideally, as we seek our most fundamental answers and identity from the One who created us. When someone implies it is their spouse's job to solve their fear, insecurity, or anger, I (Michael) am quick to point out that each of us must fight our *own* battle against insecurity. Winning that struggle is on us, not our spouse.

INSECURITY

And yet as each of us looks at our spouse, out fighting their own battle, we provide them *ammunition*—on the side of confidence or on the side of insecurity. Speaking life into each other's area of deep vulnerability is a God-given opportunity to affirm one another well.

And this, of course, is where we need to bring in sex.

> **TRUTH #2:** Sex—and the process of getting there—may mean something different to our spouse

Given these inner realities, sex, and the context into which it fits, has an emotional meaning that goes far beyond the physical act. Through all our words and actions that lead up to a time of intimacy, and during sex itself, we are speaking directly to the vulnerability in our spouse and sending a message: Yes, you are loveable. Or no, you really aren't. Yes, you are able. Or no, not so much.

> Sex, and the context into which it fits, has an emotional meaning that goes far beyond the physical act. We are speaking directly to the vulnerability in our spouse and sending a message.

There are many individual differences, but overall, here's what we tend to be longing to feel:

- Women: *I want to feel cherished, loved, immensely appealing, close to you, and that you are paying close attention to me.*

- Men: *I want to feel wanted, appreciated, immensely desirable, close to you, and that you can't keep your hands off me.*

We both deeply want to feel close to one another. But the *order* of intimacy that most creates that connection may be different for each of us. As we approach our spouse for sexual connection or they approach us, these are often our subconscious thoughts:

- Women tend to think: *We can do that once you touch my heart.*

- Men tend to think: *You touch my heart by doing that.*

Regardless of who has higher or lower desire, men of all desire levels are roughly twice as likely as women of all desire levels to say sex would most touch their heart after a hard day. Women were much more likely than men to say that listening and asking questions would do so.[5] (Both men and women were more likely to choose listening overall—although many men in the interviews were quick to indicate they meant "before sex," not "instead of sex"!)

But what happens if instead of touching our spouse's vulnerable heart, we hit it like a raw nerve?

- If women are hurt: They tend to withdraw sexually.
- If men are hurt: They tend to withdraw emotionally.

And finally, what happens if we *do* touch our spouse's heart in the way they are longing for?

- When a woman's heart is cared for: She is more likely to be more sexually open, sensual, and playful.
- When a man's heart is cared for: He is more likely to be emotionally warm, attentive, and tender.

These four sets of patterns are significant generalizations. How it works in *your* individual relationship will be impacted by many factors beyond gender, including who has initiating or receptive desire, who has what temperament, and so on. But the overall patterns are clear from years of research and clinical practice.

Let's take a deeper dive into just one common aspect of these truths for each gender, speaking directly to each spouse as we do so.

TRUTH #3: Women are more likely to feel that "sex begins in the kitchen"[6]

Men, that phrase captures a key reality for the 73 percent of women with receptive desire (as mentioned in chapter 4): Your attention to her *outside* the bedroom, throughout the day (including in the kitchen over breakfast), sets the stage for her interest in your attention *inside* the bedroom. You can see this is not about jumping through hoops to get the prize. As you do things that give your wife a positive answer to the "Am I loveable?" question—for example, as you hold her hand or text her "you're beautiful"—she feels cared for. It helps her feel close to you.

One man gave a great example:

> For thirty years I probably haven't been great at listening. But my wife was unhappy and finally told me, "I don't want you to just go through the motions of asking about my day. . . . I want you to *want* to know about my day!" So even though my brain doesn't work this way, I started looking for opportunities to say, "Tell me all about it." If she had a tense meeting with her boss: "Tell me all about it." Or if she seemed worried about our grandkids being bullied. She felt so loved by that, and it really *worked* to bring us together.

One woman captured the longing of many: "How can I get my husband to truly understand that I would want sex

INSECURITY

more if he would connect with me emotionally and make me feel cherished?"

Connecting outside the bedroom is even more important if your wife has receptive desire or lower desire than you do. Remember, people with receptive desire often must *choose* to engage sexually before they feel aroused. That choice is usually based on how you've made your spouse feel the rest of the day. One of our advisors, Angie Landry, a sex therapist in the Nashville area,[7] explained it to me (Shaunti) this way:

> All sorts of experiments have found that our *perception* about someone creates reality. As a simplistic example, what a wife thinks about her husband and his intentions are stored in a more instinctive area of the brain, the mid-brain. The fight-or-flight system accesses that area to know how to respond to him. So if the wife sees that her husband is listening well or extending affirming touch, then her perceptions and memories are positive. Her fight-or-flight system is probably calmed down and her body is able to function from a place of safety. Her perceptions actually change her, physically. She is far more able and willing to lean in to him, to want to have sex.

As one woman put it, "I know that my body climaxing almost has more to do with how close I feel to my husband than it does the physical act."

And of course, the reverse is true. If your wife feels like there *isn't* an emotional closeness and bond, it becomes much harder to connect physically. One woman that I (Shaunti) interviewed anonymously over Zoom was very blunt:

> If he's not listening or valuing me during the day, then I don't want him to put his arms around me at night. Because what he's doing is *untrue*. That affection feels like a farce. And that goes both ways. If I'm being critical or condescending to him and then say, "Let's get into bed," he wouldn't like that either.

TRUTH #4: Men are more likely to feel that sex brings closeness—and become more affectionate as a result

INSECURITY

Ladies, it is easy to think of the drive for sex as being primarily physical for men, but the *importance* of sex in your man's life is probably much more about an emotional need. Two truths are key.

First, sex for your husband probably isn't just about the physical act—it is also about *feeling that you desire him*. Feeling desired speaks reassurance at a very deep level to his hidden insecurities. When it comes to sex, "Does she think I am able?" takes on a whole new meaning! And his question is not just "Am I desirable?" but "Am I desirable to *her*?"

If he's like most men, your husband is probably longing to sense that you *want* him. In the research with men for *For Women Only*, fully 97 percent of men said getting all the sex they wanted wouldn't matter if they didn't also feel desired by their wives.

A positive answer to those questions likely has a profound impact. For 77 percent of men, feeling desired gives him a sense of confidence and well-being far beyond the bedroom and into *every other area of his life*.

Men: Imagine that your wife was an interested and motivated sexual partner, and you therefore had an active love life. How would that affect your emotional state?	
It would have little or no effect–sex seems unrelated to my emotions or how I feel about the rest of my life.	23%
It would have a positive effect–it would give me a greater sense of well-being and satisfaction with life.	77%

Source: *For Women Only.* Question shortened.

"What is with men and sex?" one female married client asked me (Michael). "No matter what is going on, it's like the cure for everything. He's depressed? I have sex with him—he's fine. Angry with the kids? I have sex with him—he's fine. Bad day at work? Sex—he's fine!" I responded with, "Listen, you are never responsible for changing him—with your body or otherwise. But it sounds like you're realizing that you actually have great power in his life. You're realizing that, if you want to, you can press the reset button on your husband any time!"[8]

Of course, the opposite is also true. His feeling *not* desired—that you're just not that interested—can result in the depressing feeling that his deep self-doubts have been confirmed. Because the emotional stakes are high, men often feel very vulnerable when they approach their wife for intimacy.

We heard that fear and need for reassurance multiplied exponentially among men who had a more specific reason for worry about being able to sexually function (due to age, trauma, medical factors, and so on). Great relief comes when a man sees that his wife still finds him desirable and is not disappointed in him.

Crucially, if a man's self-doubt has been *confirmed*—if he feels incapable or inadequate at anything, not just sex—he often *finds it very hard to try*. He shuts down and withdraws. But a man who is reassured is far more likely to keep working and trying to be the man he wants to be—for you.

A second key truth is that sex likely helps your man feel close to you. If he feels disconnected from you, if he senses distance during the day, he may reach out for you sexually to address that discomfort. You may think it is crazy that he wants sex when you are at odds—and not realize that he is reaching for you *because* you are at odds! When he has an orgasm with you, oxytocin (a bonding hormone) is released in his brain and he feels close to you again.

For example, suppose your husband has been at a work convention in Las Vegas for a week. He comes home and wants

INSECURITY

to make love. You may be thinking, *He spent the whole week in Vegas looking at these other women and he's all aroused and is bringing that home to me. That doesn't feel good.*

But what if in his mind and heart, he's instead been missing you all week and feeling disconnected? If so, he knows that in fifteen minutes he can feel completely connected to you. At the moment of his climax, his oxytocin goes up more than 500 percent.[9] He is feeling 110 percent connected to you. But if you engage in sex solely as a duty, you might not feel even 1 percent more connected. Because for you, perhaps it would have been more valuable if he had taken you to dinner, asked what it's been like caring for the kids solo all week, and nurtured you a bit.

All that said, if it is a *positive* sexual experience for you, oxytocin is released in your body and creates bonding feelings for you as well. In most cases, it is vital for both of you. But that hormonal rush truly does have a unique power, emotionally, in a man's life. One man captured it well:

> There was a season my wife was busy and not thinking about sex, so I didn't feel connected. And I couldn't articulate why I was sad. Finally, I was able to say, "I'm lonely." She understood. And everything changed.

Crucially, when a man feels close, he's more likely to *act* close. Many women have noticed that a man who might have been stressed or distant becomes more affectionate in the day or two after they make love. Not long ago, I (Shaunti) was speaking at a women's conference and mentioned this topic. A woman told me afterward:

> My husband is reserved, and I used to get upset if he didn't hug me at other times. But then I noticed that if we would make love, the next day he *was* hugging me. Or he would scoot me closer to him while we were watching TV. I love that so much. And it wasn't because he wanted sex that night, because I have a forty-eight-hour rule! I've told him how much that stuff matters to me, but I think he's mostly doing it because he's *feeling* more affectionate toward me.

If you've seen this, you're not imagining it. A man's levels of oxytocin, vasopressin, prolactin, dopamine, and other chemicals are all higher after having sex, and flood him with positive feelings for you.

INSECURITY

TRUTH #5: Other insecurities can impact how we feel about sex

Trauma, medical issues, depression, relational troubles, childhood hang-ups, and many other insecurities impact our emotions around marriage and sex. People dealing with those worries ("Am I going to be able to climax?" "I don't want to be with her when I'm so depressed." "Is he thinking about that other woman he saw walking by?") may avoid sex.

Because both partners are impacted, both have a role to play in healing. The partner who is avoiding sex has a responsibility to work on themselves and get professional help when necessary. Their spouse may need to be particularly empathetic and patient, willing to look at the long game, and willing to learn relevant details and work on themselves as well.

Showing each other you care is a huge part of moving toward healing. As one husband put it, "Realizing that I could trust my wife and actually tell her when I was struggling with this particular issue was so important. And it has created so much more intimacy."

So how do we create security, to connect sexually?

In part because of our vulnerabilities, each of us values and wants intimacy. A few key steps will help.

- *Learn your spouse—and yourself.* You are not statistics. You're individuals. So learn *your spouse's* insecurities and needs. Then commit to avoid jabbing at their painful nerve and to building them up instead. It is also crucial to understand *yourself.* Your spouse probably *wants* to care for you well, and learning about you will help them be successful. Of course, creating a great marriage and intimate life will never come from focusing on what our spouse should be doing and trying to get our needs met. But as we work on ourselves and learn how to care for our spouse well, that hopefully creates space that invites them into the work. While not a given, it is often the fruit of our labors.

- *Practice.* Wherever we have differences, the words and actions that matter most to our spouse may not feel like second nature to us. For example, many women have said they often think appreciative thoughts, but the words "Thank you" or "Good job" don't always trip off their tongue. Men frequently think how thankful they are for their wife, but have to be purposeful about saying, "I'm so grateful you married me." Thankfully, with practice the words and actions that matter are more likely to come naturally.

- *Talk about what matters—in a solutions-focused way.* Learning gets easier when you don't have to guess. Which usually means talking about it. Don't let a concern about your spouse's insecurity keep you from speaking up. Just do it kindly and with a focus on the solution rather than the problem. For example, we are pretty sure saying "I need you to give me more sex" will make things worse! But if you say instead, "Sex fills me up, and I really desire to be close to you," then there's an opening.

- *Care for the underlying emotions—especially when the answer is no.* In general, the spouse giving the no should try to sandwich it between encouraging statements and a proposal. ("Sweetheart, I would love to be with you. I'm sorry I'm grumpy after dealing with teenage attitudes all day. Can we try this Friday night?") The spouse being turned down needs to practice not seeing it as a rejection of them. (More on this in chapter 8.)

Get encouragement and support from others. Every marriage needs support: consistent fellowship with others who care and can come alongside when needed. Just be sure it is someone supportive of your spouse and your marriage. It is easy to join in complaining if you're around those who rag on their own spouses. Instead, turn toward people who help you see the good in your spouse.

The effort will make a difference

What we're suggesting in this chapter may require a personal commitment to see and care for the inner life of your spouse in a way that may not come naturally at first. But the effort to learn how is worth it.

Learning requires a sense of curiosity—which is game-changing when applied to our sex life. Let's look at that fascinating truth next.

7

the magic touch

*how a curious approach
is a sexual superpower*

> **THE SURPRISE:** Curiosity and playfulness make sex more erotic and emotionally meaningful than perfect technique.

magine three kids entering a playroom. One makes a bee-line to the toys they always play with and doesn't look at anything else. The second child is haughty and critical of each toy and task in the room. The face of the third shows delight and wonder as they try old toys and explore new ones. When something doesn't work, they don't get irritated or back off. Instead, they get an, *I wonder if* . . . look on their face and examine it in a different way.

If you could choose just *one* of those kids as a playmate, which one would you choose? More important, if you had to *be* one of those three children, which would you choose to be?

Most of us would want the curious friend, not the one on autopilot, and certainly not the critical one. Most of us can also see that *being* the curious one is a lot more fun.

This realization can change everything when we apply it to the adult version of that situation.

Inquiring Minds Want to Know

Curiosity has an almost miraculous power in marriage, and in our intimate lives. It can help us build something beautiful. And it doesn't matter what our background, our IQ, or our level of education is. As Albert Einstein once explained, "I have no special talents. I am only passionately curious."[1]

Curiosity is a thirst to know or learn something. Once you cultivate the desire to learn the intimate things that make your spouse tick, you will see that curiosity truly is a sexual superpower. A simple, sincere, inquisitive approach to your spouse can be even more impactful than a vast array of sexual knowledge or perfect technique.

One of my (Michael's) friends describes his wife's body as "Disneyland with skin on . . . a new theme park to explore every day." I love that mindset—for any spouse. He is always struck with wonder and amazement when he looks at her. "To be honest," he also said, "occasionally I'm stuck in the haunted house for a couple days, but even that can be an adventure if I roll with it."

If you think about it, in every interaction in life, we are operating based on one of three stances: clueless, critical, or curious. Clueless is where we spend much of our time: We go about our routine without wondering about those around us. Sometimes, though, things are challenging, and we can slip into a critical stance: We are seeing things around us, all right, but it is mostly what we're dissatisfied with! The curious stance is completely different and is the antidote to the other two: It is an attitude of leaning in, being open, even inquisitive. It becomes a mindset.

Yet because curiosity is powerful, we must also remember the famous advice Uncle Ben gave Peter Parker (Spider-Man): "With great power comes great responsibility."[2] While curiosity can be beautiful, there is a potential dark side. If we focus it just on self, it can become selfish, rebellious, and unhealthy. If we don't have healthy boundaries, it can lead us into territory that is infectious and destructive (e.g., exploring dark recesses online).

A healthy curiosity is focused on continually discovering your spouse—and working to understand them. To *learn* them. What matters to your spouse most, in and out of the bedroom? What do they really enjoy and what do they merely

CURIOSITY

tolerate? What have they avoided telling you because they are worried it will hurt your feelings?

Curiosity means sincerely trying to find the answers to those sorts of questions. And we almost always can.

Curiosity Matters

That effort is worth it. On our survey (MIS),[3] whether a spouse viewed their partner as sexually curious had a striking impact on many aspects of that couple's intimate life. Here are a few key implications.

> **FINDING #1:** Sincere curiosity stirs up a host of positive sex and marriage outcomes

It's easy to see benefits flowing from someone's sincere desire to learn about their spouse: not just more understanding, but more enjoyment in the relationship, a more vibrant intimate life, the healing of hurts, and so on.

Yet only about half (52 percent) of our survey-takers viewed their spouse as generally "open, inviting, and curious" about what they enjoyed sexually. Everyone else felt their spouse was just not quite there: either sometimes curious and other times not so much, or even clueless or selfish.

Do you believe your spouse is generally curious about what you do and don't enjoy, sexually? (Choose one.)	
Yes, my spouse generally stays open, inviting and curious about my preferences.	52%
My spouse is sometimes open, sometimes not so much.	27%
I think my spouse is sometimes just clueless.	9%
No, it seems like my spouse's focus is on what they want and they don't tend to explore what I would like.	8%
No, they seem to believe that their way is right (or mine is wrong), so there is no need to ask.	4%

Source: MIS, n=1097

And there is clearly a benefit to curiosity.[4] For example, if your spouse views you as curious about what matters to them sexually, you are more than *three times* as likely to have a very happy marriage than if your spouse views you as less than curious. (Among those who were happy in marriage, 60 percent said they had curious spouses, compared with just 17 percent among those unhappy in marriage.) Similarly, if your spouse views you as curious, you *both* are more than three times as likely to be very happy with how often you have sex.

In fact, the more your spouse views you as curious, the more often you are likely to have sex, period! Take a look at the crazy graphic on the next page!

Also, remember our earlier discussion (chapter 5) that having sex once a week (or more) appears to be a tipping

Sexual frequency and curiosity

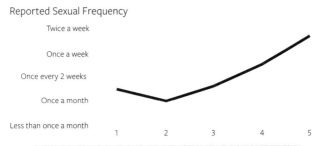

Reported Sexual Frequency

Twice a week

Once a week

Once every 2 weeks

Once a month

Less than once a month

1   2   3   4   5

1: No, they seem to believe that their way is right (or mine is wrong), so there is no need to ask.

2: No, it seems like my spouse's focus is on what they want and they don't tend to explore what I would like.

3: I think my spouse is sometimes just clueless.

4: My spouse is sometimes open, sometimes not so much.

5: Yes, my spouse generally stays open, inviting and curious about my preferences.

Source: MIS n=1097

point for several positive outcomes—perhaps even including a positive cycle of *wanting* to have sex? Well, if your spouse views you as curious, you as a couple are more than three times as likely to reach that weekly tipping point, or go beyond it. Conversely, if your spouse views you as *less* than curious, you are 3.5 times more likely to be in a low-sex/no-sex marriage.

The encouragement to become sincerely curious and learn your spouse is clear!

FINDING #2: Curiosity is one of the most direct ways of showing that you care—just as lack of curiosity signals the opposite

Time and again in our interviews and surveys with those dissatisfied in their marriage and sex life, we heard comments like this: "I've told him three times that I don't like it when he does that, but he seems to just be in a routine and doesn't remember. I can still try to get myself in the mood, but it puts a damper on things. I want it to be important enough for him to remember." Or the forty-year-old man who said, "She only wants to do same-old, same-old. She's indifferent to anything else."

The message being received by routine, lack of remembering, or indifference is clear: *I'm not curious about you . . . and don't really care about you.* That perception may not be true at all, but that is what these spouses are hearing.

By contrast, among those who *praised* their spouse, we frequently heard how "considerate" their spouse was sexually. And by definition, being considerate is nearly synonymous with knowing and acting on what matters to the other person—which requires curiosity to begin with. Look at the comments from this pastor and his wife.

HER: When things got hard two years ago, we knew something had to change. He changed jobs, we lost

CURIOSITY

a baby, we weren't communicating, there was a lot of misunderstanding and hurt. Especially about sex. We were both wondering about each other, sexually, and wanting to understand each other, but didn't know how to get started.

HIM: We got a marriage book that would give us an excuse to talk about the sexual stuff. We'd been married for fifteen years and had five kids, but that was the first time we'd talked about the physical things we do. And suddenly we discovered things! Like, we finally talked about this one sexual thing that we both felt we "should" like—and found out that neither of us did! It relieved a lot of anxiety.

HER: I felt more freedom to say, "That isn't good for me," or "That feels good, but go left." I could tell that he *wanted* to know what mattered to me. We started to feel intimate again—and not just sexually.

HIM: We were like, why didn't we do this fifteen years ago?

A curious approach allows you to consider problems with grace and a sense of anticipation. ("What will I learn about us and our bodies this time?") For example, if your wife seems unaroused, rather than pulling away because you feel like you failed, you accept the challenge and curiously ask what might work. Or if your husband seems passive, you neither pull back nor overcompensate. Instead, you curiously ask, "What's up?" What would help him want to engage?

> **FINDING #3:** Curiosity reduces anxiety and makes sex more playful and erotic

Your curiosity about what sexually delights your spouse creates an important dynamic: It allows you to relax a bit. It makes space for playfulness. And that relaxed, exploratory, playful feeling is itself powerfully erotic. This is one of the reasons some spouses eventually *want* to engage in certain sexual acts they used to avoid—because it brings their spouse so much delight!

A while back, I (Michael) was counseling a couple who had a lot of disappointments sexually. The husband had always hoped his wife would be willing to perform oral sex, and she didn't feel competent. As she told me, "I don't know how. I feel clumsy. And I feel like he's comparing me to previous partners." Even though he insisted that he loved being with her in that way, she was bound up by anxiety.

He was not pressuring her, and she was not truly opposed to the idea—just afraid. Because they both wanted to move forward, I suggested she consider shifting the way she

CURIOSITY

thought about it from a fear-based "I don't know how" mindset to a curious "I wonder" mindset. I suggested that the next time they were intimate, she use it as an opportunity not to try to "do" oral sex and "get it right," but to play. To discover. To explore. Does this feel good? What happens when I do *this*? He looked excited, and her face immediately shifted to a curious look as she considered how that would work.

"That right there," I said. "That feeling you're having is curiosity. You're considering what it would be like to approach it differently. If you can hang on to that feeling through the play, you can at least discover if you like it." She ended up enjoying it once it became about exploring with no expectations.

Taking the pressure off a sexual experience is important. Curiosity feels much better than anxiety. Especially because it makes room for playfulness. Fully 80 percent of survey-takers said it increased their sexual enjoyment when their spouse was playful. As one man said, "I'm higher-desire than my wife and would like to make love more often, but in my mind, one really playful sexual encounter per week is better than two iffy ones."

Your curiosity helps your spouse feel safe, which is what allows for playfulness to happen. The spouses mentioned here would not have been able to explore or have a playful sexual encounter if they didn't feel safe with their spouse.

> **FINDING #4:** Curiosity keeps things fresh and allows you to notice things you might have missed

Because people secretly worry about it as the years go by, every sex-advice column offers a constant stream of advice about "How to keep sex fresh and exciting." The good news is, things *won't* get boring in the bedroom if you're being inquisitive and keeping an eye open for the evolution of what matters to your spouse! This advice is not nearly as spicy as "Five ways to use whipped cream in bed"—but it is far more practical and will help you for the rest of your lives.

You and your spouse will evolve over the years. Getting into a rut often simply means a couple is no longer curious about each other. Through smaller changes (your spouse is in a tiring season with kids) and big ones (you have a major work schedule change), each of us has to stay open to the question, "What is important to my spouse right now that I need to know?"

CURIOSITY

Each of us has to stay open to the question, "What is important to my spouse right now that I need to know?"

As you do, you may also find out certain encouraging things! In one interview, a long-married wife exclaimed, "I only recently learned that he now liked to cuddle! I was always the cuddler and he just wanted sex, and so I avoided *both* sometimes. And now I suddenly hear that after thirty-three years of marriage, he actually *likes* cuddling. I wouldn't have believed it, but this was valuable information!"

> **FINDING #5:** Demonstrating curiosity is simpler than you may think

Curiosity is a simple skill to build—it is mostly a *mindset* that becomes a habit. It starts with a humility that acknowledges you don't know it all . . . and you especially don't know everything about your spouse. This fosters a willingness to keep your eyes open and try to figure out answers over time.

Remember the forty-year-old husband who said his wife "only wants to do same-old, same-old" things in the bedroom, and seemed "indifferent" to all else? Imagine the difference it would make if, instead of continuing in his confusion and disappointment, he were to make it his goal to uncover *why* his wife always wanted to do "same old, same old." So he asks a question or two. ("Honey, I'm wondering; when I wanted to try that thing the other night, you seemed a bit tense. Can you tell me what you were thinking or worried about in the moment? . . . Oh, you were uncomfortable?") Maybe he observes his wife and her reactions. (*Hmm . . . when I do* this *she says she enjoys it; when I do* that *she tenses up.*)

What if in the process he were to discover that his wife's reluctance has nothing to do with indifference and lack of caring and everything to do with a common fear among those for whom the ability to climax feels like a touch-and-go thing. As one wife told me (Shaunti), "It's easy for my husband to come. It's not easy for me. He needs to work at getting me to that point, but now that we've figured out *what* works, I want to keep doing that! He wants to experiment so much more— but when we do, I have a lot of anxiety about whether I'm going to get there. And sometimes I don't. So experimenting might be fun for him, but it's just not as enjoyable for me."

If the newly curious husband discovers his wife has a similar anxiety, he has an entirely new perspective on what is going on. He no longer assumes that she is indifferent to what matters to him. Even better, his asking about it shows his wife that he cares, and bonds them together. If he also feels safe enough to discuss what matters to *him*, they will be drawn even closer.

CURIOSITY

So How Do We Get Curious?

Clearly there are benefits to a lifetime of curiosity. So what's the best way to get there? Here are a few key tips.

- *Be humble and honest with yourself: Would your spouse say you need to move from clueless or critical to curious?* Look at the opening survey chart on page 159 and ask yourself where your spouse would place you.

On one survey, a wife said the one thing she wished her husband knew was "How much non-sexual soft touch (hand holding, hugs, back rubs) is important to initiate sex for me, and how much I wish he would do that." Sure enough, in her other survey answers she indicated her spouse wasn't particularly curious. So the question for you is: What things matter to *your* spouse that you are not aware of? Then *apply* what you learn.

Ask questions. This doesn't mean an inquisition—that's intimidating, not inviting. True curiosity produces open space in a relationship. Think of a truly curious child, not your critical sister-in-law trying to trap you. So if you don't quite understand something, pursue the question. (Usually later, not in the moment. For example: "Last night, I'm wondering why you pulled away when I did such-and-such? I thought you liked that?")

Hopefully you will learn something useful. ("I do like it, but if you do it over and over it becomes a bit sensitive and irritating; I'd rather you do that a few times and then move on to *this* instead.") But even if your spouse isn't comfortable talking about it, you can always try different things and observe the results. Play around. See what delights your spouse.

■ *If you need help talking, read a book out loud together.* Take turns reading and use the book as the excuse to talk about sexual things. One wife said, "I've been reluctant to share certain things because I want to give him affirmation rather than making him feel like I'm being critical: 'Try this, not that.' But when we finally read a book together, it was like, 'Now this isn't personal. We're being invited into this conversation; we can blame it on the author!' We were suddenly tackling a problem *together* and were on the same page working it out."

■ *Help your spouse be curious about you.* Stephen Covey's fifth habit of highly effective people is "Understand to be understood."[5] After you have been curious about your spouse, if you think they would be open to it, ask if they would like to hear from you. This has to be sincere. Pretending to be curious to get what you want will typically encourage your spouse to shut down, not open up!

"So Much More Intimacy Comes from Trying"

Even though our efforts to be curious will be imperfect, they are worth trying. In one interview, a husband captured well the power of trying to figure things out:

> I think it was A.W. Tozer who said something like, "God knows we cannot begin to understand His true nature but

He loves the fact that we try, in whatever capacity we can."
And I'm hoping it is sort of the same with my wife. My
hope is that even though I try and fumble about and ask
silly questions and try again, that she would give me grace
in that effort, even though I'm a twit. There's mystery to
her that I'm not sure I'll fully understand, but so much more
intimacy comes from trying.

getting started

*why real connection comes more
from the right signals than the right moves*

THE SURPRISE: Having a comfortable way to signal (and receive) openness or interest will create connection and prevent much pain.

onday evening. Nate got home from work at 6 p.m., gave Sonya a hug, and dashed upstairs to change before taking their middle-school boys to basketball. He then ducked into the master bathroom and checked an unobtrusive corner of the mirror. On it, written in dry erase marker, was "4." He shrugged, hurried back downstairs, smiled at his wife, loaded up the boys, and headed out.

Tuesday evening. Nate's wife was at her shift as a pharmacist, so he got the boys dinner and got them started on their homework. At 8:15, Sonya walked in looking very tired and went to change. When he checked, the mirror had "2" on it. He suggested they snuggle on the couch and watch their latest TV binge together. She fell asleep with her head on his shoulder.

Wednesday evening. Nate got home at 8 p.m., after a testy meeting at work. He dragged himself upstairs. The mirror had "9" on it. A smile spread across his face. When he got back to the kitchen, he hugged the boys and looked over their shoulders to his wife. She gave him an impish look. And about two hours later, they were feeling amazing.

This is a true story about a real couple who have discovered how to unlock one of the most unrecognized but most important skills a couple can have in their intimate life: knowing how to initiate sex.

Sparking the Flame

You may have read that last sentence and thought, *What do you mean, we need to know how to initiate sex? Don't you just do it?!*

Well, it turns out that one of the sneakiest reasons for disappointment or hurt (when we don't connect well or as often as we want) or pressure (when we feel we are disappointing our spouse) is that we don't know the best way of *starting* to "do it."

If you were going to be a contestant on a reality TV survival show, you would never show up without having figured out how you were going to start a fire, right? Would you be allowed to bring a butane lighter? Would you use a ferro rod? Or would you have to learn the exhausting friction method of sparking kindling? No matter what, you would sort through what *actually*, technically, you would do to spark the fire, then build skill in doing that well.

It turns out, we need to do the same thing in the bedroom.

Nate and Sonya are the stereotypical couple where he has both higher desire and initiating desire. She is a receptive-desire person, and her temperament is such that she really, *really* doesn't want to have to initiate. They eventually realized it takes a whole lot of pressure off if she has a way of signaling her level of receptivity, and he has a way of knowing what to expect.

Thus, the mirror score. Most days, she signals the answer to this question: "On a scale of 1 to 10, how receptive am I feeling today?" (He was originally going to signal how much he felt like initiating, but quickly realized he was always in the 8 to 10 range!) An 8 to 10 was her way of saying, "I'm a sure bet, if you ask." Anything under 5 was a range from "Doubtful" to "Stay back if you'd like to keep your parts." And those middle numbers—5, 6, and 7—provided her most

INITIATION

crucial signal: "I'm not sure. But if you play it right, I *might* be able to start feeling it."

Figuring out *how* we signal each other so that we can connect well—or, conversely, *not* connect and yet still do *that* well—is what this chapter is about.

How Do We Initiate?

Many of us have not thought about what *actually* gets the process of sex started. We don't have a clear, mutually appealing way of showing that we're interested or up for it—or not. So when there's a sense of disappointment, pressure, or frustration ("I never know what answer I'm going to get"), we tend to think the issue is about someone's sex drive (or lack thereof). When in reality, it may be about *initiation*.

> When there's a sense of disappointment, pressure, or frustration, the issue may not be about our sex drives but about *initiation*.

During one interview with me (Shaunti) and Jeff, a couple got into a bit of an argument about who was higher desire. The husband insisted his wife was, and she said that she didn't think so; she was just frustrated by his actions (or lack thereof).

Suddenly, the husband said, "Hold on," and there was a long pause while the two of them seemed to be consulting (remember, we did this via Zoom with their video off). Then the husband said, "I think she's right. I probably *am* higher desire—but she's more apt to take the step of actually initiating. Like, if I text her, 'What's for dinner?' she might text back, 'You.' And that gets me thinking about it. Huh. I guess I need to think more about initiating, since I probably *do* want sex more than she does!"

Once we figure out the skills, it is amazing how much freedom and pleasure it brings to our intimate relationship. Suddenly, things flow much more easily. But before we start, there is one critical foundation we must build.

Setting the Foundation: Being Seductive

Have you ever forgotten to bring in wood for a fire, and instead left it out in the rain? I (Shaunti) have. After speaking at a winter women's event in Vermont, I had a two-day break before another one. My amazing hosts insisted on putting me up in a beautiful little cabin with a fireplace and a supply of wood out back. I quickly built a crackling fire for the evening.

My hosts recommended bringing in the firewood for the next day, as it had been a rainy winter, but I was cozy and figured I would get it in the morning. I was picturing a woodshed out back, but as I discovered the next freezing morning, it was a wood *pile*. On that cold, wet morning, every log I put on the fire sputtered and smoked. No matter what I did, the firewood would not catch.

Trying to spark sex without living seductively first is like trying to light a fire with a batch of wood that is damp instead of dry.

The word *seduction* can raise some eyebrows. We might think of it as manipulating someone against their will. But that's not how it works. And that is not how we're using the word here. Seduction isn't something you do *to* someone. It always requires both an invitation *and* a response. If someone is not open, there's no seduction.

Similarly, seduction needs to be more than a one-time attempt to charm; true seduction requires living in a way that always cares for and appeals to your spouse. Putting on your skimpy outfit and walking in front of your husband might be a seductive stereotype, but may not work if you're not *living* seductively.

Living seductively means bringing your best self to the party

When we are dating, most of us instinctively understand living seductively. We seek to be our best. We show up intentionally and well. We think through our clothing, our hair; we put on a smile, are thoughtful and considerate. We do everything we can to draw in this other person and woo them into choosing us.

But something often happens after the wedding. We may shift to a mindset of "This is what you chose . . . deal with it." We stop insisting we be our best around the person we say is the most important to us. Instead, we allow them to interact with our worst self, while work and friends get a better version of us. Then we wonder why the sexual spark doesn't work.

While we can *do* seductive things, the key is *living* it. It means bringing your best self to the party, day after day, with attention and care to your spouse, rather than just going through the motions or even allowing yourself to be unpleasant. After all, in each of us there is a part that wants to please our spouse—and a part that is selfish, lazy, tired, or really doesn't give a rip right now. Every day we have to decide: Which me am I going to be?

And then we need to know what to *do* with the "good me." We need to know—and focus on—what our *spouse* finds seductive. Especially since what we find seductive may not have much impact on our spouse. For example, many a husband has had to come to terms with the fact that his wife is turned on by watching him tumble on the floor with the kids and *not* by watching him strut around naked after his shower. (For grief counseling, see the next chapter.)

Similarly, many a higher-desire wife has recognized that what unlocks her husband's interest starts with words of affirmation rather than words of love.

In an interview with one busy couple, the wife described her husband often doing sweet things specifically for her. Now, some women have told us they are skeptical of those actions and see them as self-serving, that he's hoping to get lucky later. But this wife did not.

The husband chimed in with one reason why. "I can tell it is *definitely* about my actions twelve to twenty-four hours in advance. If I'm distracted for days, come home, put the kids to bed, and then expect to snuggle, I'm going to be sleeping in the guest room! But it changes things when I regularly send her a text message in the middle of day. Or like, she called this afternoon and I took time to listen, even though there was a lot going on and it was busy."

As pointed out above, we also have to be *open* to being seduced, under that crucial principle of—in a marriage of goodwill—believing the best of our spouse's intentions toward us. When our survey respondents were polled about their motivations for doing sweet things in the explicit hopes of "getting lucky later," 79 percent had generally unselfish motivations (like, "This will take a load off my spouse's plate, which will make it easier for them to want to have sex later") or said that doing nice things had nothing to do with whether they wanted to get lucky later! Only 17 percent had potentially self-focused motivations. (For example, 9 percent recognized that they didn't do these things enough and used the thought of wanting sex as a prompt to be attentive.)[1]

Thankfully, the vast majority of survey-takers (71 percent) said they also assumed that their spouse's "hoping to get lucky" efforts were sincere. Just 13 percent thought something negative.

If you suspect your spouse is doing something they don't usually do (giving you a neck massage, picking up after the kids, etc.) because they are hoping to get lucky later, how do you feel about that? (Choose all that apply)	
I'm okay with it!	44%
I'm okay with it, with conditions (such as that my spouse doesn't pout if they don't get sex)	27%
I view it as selfish/only happening when my spouse wants to get lucky	4%
I am NOT okay with it—my spouse doesn't care about me, they just want sex	4%
Does not apply; my spouse would not be thinking about getting lucky later	16%
Does not apply; my spouse does not do nice things like that	5%

Source: MIS, n=1097
Question and answers paraphrased and categorized.

Living seductively means fighting our worst tendencies

Living seductively also means *not* letting your worst self come out with your spouse. For example, maybe you realize you have to stop treating your spouse like another child to be managed, or fight off irritation that they didn't notice the work you put in on the lawn. Maybe you fight the temptation to be

INITIATION

cold in bed because you're hanging on to anger about something your spouse said over breakfast, or to act like a martyr when your spouse asks you to run an errand when you're tired.

And you know you can fight your less-than-appealing natural tendencies because you already do. For example, you seduce people at work every day.

Yeah, that sounds funny. But when you're at work (or at church, or homeschooling the kids, or planning the retirement community event), you don't demand the things you want. You *seduce* them from your colleagues, your friends, or whomever you are with. You know being exasperated or pouty would *not* be appealing. So you bring your best self to the party, and draw the best out of others.

We need to apply the same skill with our spouse.

Once we are living seductively, the environment is set. We are drawing each other into space prepped for more intimate connection. Which leads us to actually initiating the event. It doesn't matter how seductive we are if someone doesn't take the step to start the sexual encounter. We call that step the *spark*. And this is where building several simple skills will make all the difference.

SKILL #1: Send a signal to create a spark

In the movies, sex is spontaneous and just happens. The couple look at each other and mutually jump into a heavy kiss while they strip each other's clothes off. But it rarely works that way in real life. Whether one is starting a car or lighting a fire, ignition doesn't happen without a spark. In this case, a spark is a *signal*—the signal you use to tell your spouse you are open or interested.

Sparks can be verbal ("Wanna get naked?") or nonverbal (beginning to caress more private areas). They can be very direct (beginning to unbutton clothing) or more indirect (taking an evening shower and not being in a hurry to get pajamas on).

Scheduled sex is a type of initiation sex therapists often recommend. Both spouses agree that, in general, they will be a sure bet during that time, which reduces anxiety. But even so, someone has to spark the actual lovemaking process. One wife explained, "For us, sex is supposed to be every Saturday morning. The night before, we always say, 'What time are we getting up?' So then in the morning I sneak out of bed, brush my teeth (I just *have* to), and then wake him up by kissing on him."

Indirect signals are most easily missed. For example, we often hear a wife say, "I don't initiate." But when asked, "Do you ever wear something more skimpy to bed?" she says, "Well . . . yes." That's just an indirect type of initiating! Similarly, one husband discovered that his wife *really* valued the fact that he tried to equally share the chores—and that if he explicitly flirted with his wife while he was doing

INITIATION

the dishes or before he went out to clean the gutters, it gave them both "anticipation time" and was their start to the sexual process—even if it happened hours later. His wife said, "Instead of foreplay, we call it choreplay."

An indirect spark could also be something signaled by a receptive-desire spouse that an initiating-desire spouse would totally miss if they didn't know to watch for it. Some people (especially initiating types) are comfortable being very direct. But many spouses (especially receptive types) may not feel comfortable doing something as overt as putting on sexy lingerie or sending a suggestive comment via text. So they will send other, more subtle signals.

One husband said, "I never have any idea if my wife is interested." To which she protested, "Well, last night I put my hand on your knee while you were watching the news!" To which the dumbfounded husband replied, "That was you *initiating*?"

If you are *not* the higher-desire and/or initiating spouse, it makes a dramatic difference if you take the lead in *showing* you are open and receptive—and in a way your spouse can see it.

As couples figure out what signals work for them, many find that they not only send these signals more purposefully, but that they have created their own private language. They are the only ones who know the story behind it, but both know exactly what they are talking about! "Wanna make some cookies?" "How about some fly fishing?" That sort of private joke can't be manufactured, but where it comes up, it is often a way to build a sense of playfulness and intimacy.

SKILL #2: Make sure the signal is not just being sent, but received well

Have you ever been on a video call where you were eloquently explaining something, only to be told that you were muted and no one could hear you? A signal can't just be sent, it also has to be received.

The vast majority of survey-takers said they definitely did things to show they were interested in or open to sex, but when we asked, "Does your spouse know to *take* it as a signal?" they were much less sure. Only about half of all respondents (52 percent) were signaling well *and* knew their spouse took it as such. And those who reported both those things were more likely to be having sex than those who didn't. Among those in low-sex/no-sex marriages (those having sex less than once a month), fully 70 percent were not signaling well (meaning they either didn't send a signal at all, or weren't sure if their spouse would *see* it as a signal), compared with 47 percent of those who were having sex regularly. (See chart on next page.)

Now, that said, since most couples are having sex, most have clearly created a process of initiation and responsiveness

INITIATION

Do you signal your spouse to show you're open to sex – and do they know to take it as a signal?

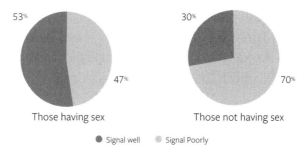

53%

47%

Those having sex

30%

70%

Those not having sex

● Signal well   ● Signal Poorly

Source: MIS, n=1097
Categories created from two questions. See research document for specifics.

that works in some way. But quite often it is working *despite* our efforts—because we care about each other and want to be intimate together—not *because* of those efforts! A few adjustments may be in order.

For example, we might need to adjust our signals to something the other person finds enticing, rather than just *wishing* it was something they would find enticing! As one leader of a sex-related ministry told me (Shaunti), "A lot of us need to shift our thinking to what our *spouse* finds erotic. For example, men can be quite focused on their equipment, but their wives are often thinking, *How about we put that away and start with the hands?*"

We may also need to investigate whether something we love doing is actually putting a speed bump in the process. When

Jeff and I (Shaunti) were interviewing spouses separately, we sometimes asked, "How do you get started?" and heard a process described. But if we asked, "Does that work for you?" quite often we heard that the person was getting in the mood *in spite of* what their spouse was used to doing. One woman said her husband would run his fingers through her long hair, which slightly tangled and pulled—which also slightly broke her concentration on the matter at hand. A man described how his wife would stroke his abdomen for quite some time, which he found immensely frustrating and *not* erotic, because he wanted her to be stroking something lower!

These little frustrations are usually not a big deal—but in most cases spouses would still want to know. One wife told me (Michael) how she always knew when her husband was trying to start sex: "Because he starts playing 'Tune in Tokyo.'" I looked confused, and she mimed the action of her husband grabbing a pair of breasts with both hands and turning them back and forth like dials.

I had to laugh. "Does that do it for you?"

She smiled and shook her head. "No. I don't mind the playfulness—I like that. I'm usually just not ready for that kind of touch right away. But he's a wonderful man and I don't want to hurt his feelings. So I just redirect him."

While her desire to be kind to her husband was admirable, I told her that it was far *more* kind in the end for her to gently share that she loved the playfulness, but his touch

INITIATION

was too direct and not seductive. Both spouses need to be able to share what they want, what they find annoying, and teach each other. Because then both can create a process that truly works, instead of discovering years later that their partner has been distracted instead of pleased all that time—or worse, being blindsided by built-up anger.

Keep in mind that these requests may need to be shared regularly and in different ways until one partner gets what the other is saying. One woman described to me (Shaunti) how her husband of twelve years had always started sexual play with a particular action, "even though I've told him multiple times that I don't like it." She had begun biting back frustration each time, thinking about how he didn't listen. She eventually began avoiding sex, even though she was actually higher desire than he was.

Sympathetically, I asked her, "How many times did you tell him that this action bothered you?"

"Like, three times."

Startled, I asked, "And when was the last time you said something?"

"Maybe five years ago. I just gave up."

In situations like that, while that husband definitely has a responsibility to listen better, it often helps for the annoyed spouse to give grace and continue to communicate their needs and desires if the other partner just doesn't get it the first few tries.

SKILL #3: Clarify what you are sparking

After a week away at a freezing construction site, Joe was looking forward to getting into his warm house, seeing his wife, Breanna, getting a late dinner, watching some mindless TV, and falling into bed. But when he finally headed to bed, Breanna came with him and began to make clear how much she had missed him all week. Joe adored his wife, but he was mentally groaning inside. "Honey—"

Breanna pulled away, hurt. Now he felt even worse. "I'm just so fried. I honestly don't know if I could do anything about it tonight." She didn't say anything, and suddenly he got an idea. "But that doesn't mean I can't do anything about *you* tonight. C'mere."

She was delighted.

The next day, he apologized again that he just couldn't hack it, and she started laughing. "I thought you hacked it great! I was just horny all week and a quickie just for me was fine."

Misunderstanding *what* is being initiated is another reason we don't always connect as well as we could.

Think about intimate touch as being divided into three categories: basic cuddling (something you could do in front of others), making out (something arousing that you wouldn't do in front of others, but not orgasm focused), and sex (orgasm focused). There is huge value in the two of you identifying language for these categories. That allows you to figure out what level of touch you are aiming for. For example: "I don't think I have the energy for sex, but I would love to cuddle."

Similarly, if one or both people are looking for actual sex, there are very different *types* of sexual connection: a quickie, a playful romp, nurturing connection, a multi-hour adventure, or a host of others. Without clarity about what is being sought, a mismatch is all too likely.

For example, perhaps the higher-desire spouse is simply looking for a cuddle . . . but their partner resists because they *assume* he or she is looking for actual sex. Maybe one partner is feeling adventurous and creative, while the other is feeling more serious after getting some difficult family news.

When you use clear language, the person who is initiating can share what they are looking for, while the other person can say, "Here's where I'm at today; I'm good up to this point." Setting such expectations and limits actually creates *freedom*. Why? Because *you don't have to guess what the other person wants*.

Once you clarify what to expect, treat it as a boundary you both will honor. That builds discipline, says, "I respect you, and I can control myself," and creates trust. It allows each spouse to relax.

SKILL #4: Know how to say and receive a no

The failure to effectively give and receive a no is one of the most infectious agents in a couple's sex life.

The key is this: Both the person who is saying no and the person who is hearing it need to convey and absorb one message—*the timing isn't right*. Because there are so many vulnerabilities and emotions involved in reaching out to a spouse sexually, it is so easy to hear painful messages in the turndown: *You aren't desirable, I don't like you, you're not appealing to me, I don't care about you.* It is highly likely that none of those is accurate, but they feel real nevertheless.

> Both the person who is saying no and the person who is hearing it need to convey and absorb one message—*the timing isn't right.*

The message *The timing isn't right* provides a reassuring alternative. That doesn't mean it doesn't sting, but it is a world away from *You aren't an appealing person.*

In general, it makes all the difference if the person giving the no can share *why* the timing isn't right and offer an alternative. In other words, "Oh honey, I'm so sorry. Today was grueling. Can we have a date Thursday after I get back from my shift?"

Similarly, the person being turned down must handle it with grace, reminding themselves that this is a timing issue. Even better, they can realize that their spouse not being ready is simply an opportunity for more attention! That will show care for their spouse and enrich the next cycle along.

It is important to note that it is okay for the receiver to have a human reaction. If they have been planning sex all day, it is understandable that hearing no would be disappointing.

However, a strong negative reaction or an overreaction (such as withdrawing or assuming something bad about the reasons for the rejection) will only cause damage. So will conveying a sense of pressure. As one woman said on the survey, "Because I know he is expecting something in return, him doing nice things for me adds a lot of pressure. Like I have to make love now that he's gone to get the oil changed and given me a back rub."

It is totally understandable that a spouse might perceive the lack of a real choice as unsettling, right? No one wants to be the cause of their spouse feeling that way.

A spouse should be able to feel totally secure in saying no, knowing that even if their partner is disappointed, they will be fine with it, won't get overly upset, and will look forward to connecting another day.

What if it seems like it is *never* the right time? Well, that is a bigger issue—and thus it becomes even more important to understand why.

So What Do We Do?

Four big-picture steps will help you implement these initiating skills well.

- *Evaluate how you live seductively—and how well.* Discuss the ways you do, and do not, seduce each other. What works? Be honest: Do you work to draw your spouse to you, or do you just expect they will be there? How can you up your seduction game?

- *Discuss your signals.* How do you know when your spouse is open or in the mood? Does that work for you? Similarly, how do you signal them when *you* are open or in the mood? Do they really know what you are signaling? Do you have language that makes it clear exactly what you would like?

  You may immediately realize that you two *do* have one or more signals that work, but you just hadn't thought of it that way before. Consider using that signal more purposefully.

- *Be creative with new ways to spark the event.* If you always use nonverbal signals, discuss verbal ways you could try.

If you are always verbally direct—"So . . . you wanna?"—discuss if there are ways to get more subtle or playful.

- *Be kind.* Much of what allows us to be intimate in the bedroom is what allows us to be intimate in our marriage overall. When it comes to receiving an approach from your spouse, or receiving their answer (including a no), care for one another with an attitude of generosity, grace, kindness, and openness.

Honor Your Spouse's Heart

A lot of vulnerability comes with sending or receiving sexual signals. Use this as an opportunity to see the heart of your spouse—the heart *underneath* that vulnerability. Not the seeming pushiness after having been gone for a week or the seeming reluctance after a long day—but the heart that is tender, that wants connection, that is often willing to try, that cares about you. *That* is what will allow you to do this dance well.

9

love the one you're with

*how a great response to disappointment
can create a great relationship*

> **THE SURPRISE:** Accepting that your spouse isn't everything you wanted lets you enjoy what you've got.

When we first decided to partner on this book, one of the things Jeff and I (Shaunti) were most excited about was the opportunity to work with an experienced therapist. We had been careful in prior books to stay in our lane and not tackle topics that should be addressed by a trained clinician.

But this partnership opened up new options! I asked Michael, "Should we investigate any of the specialized issues that Jeff and I can't usually address?"

"Like what?" he asked.

Displaying my keen grasp of therapeutic interventions, I said, "I don't know . . . anything counseling-y."

"Like some of the hard topics that impact our sex lives?" he asked. "Abuse, trauma, depression, medical problems, addiction, and so on? If we start down that road, this will be a three-thousand-page book, and still wouldn't cover those issues properly."

Jeff chimed in. "Is there any common denominator that will help struggling couples build a great relationship no matter what their issue is? That's probably too much to hope for."

Michael smiled. "Actually, every experienced counselor already knows what that common denominator is. In the end, all counseling work is grief work. Something about your spouse isn't what you were hoping for. You have to grieve what isn't and accept what is before you can move forward to enjoy what you have."

When the Long Journey Isn't the Road You Wanted

There is power in acceptance. It can transform what could be ongoing disappointment into contentment and even enjoyment.

Each of us is married to an imperfect person, and our spouse is married to an imperfect person. The best partner probably provides about 80 percent of what we would want in a spouse. We all fall short; we all have opportunities for disappointment.

Maybe you have always envisioned sex being playful, but your spouse treats it like an engineering problem. Or you've wished your spouse would sexually flirt with you during the day, but they're in work or parenting mode all day and it doesn't cross their mind.

Or perhaps there's something more significant. Maybe you feel your spouse should be much better at something that really matters to you, and because they aren't, you feel discontented or frustrated. Maybe they are struggling with behavior that you deeply wish didn't exist, but which seems unlikely to change. Or maybe you're in a neurodiverse marriage—for example, with a spouse who has ADHD or is on the autism spectrum—and their scattered focus or difficulty empathizing keeps you feeling like you are only seen in glances.

When we feel those very real disappointments, there is a way forward. It's just probably not the answer we are hoping for. We want the cause of the disappointment to be resolved, so we get everything as we want it. Instead, we must grapple with a different solution: grieving the loss of what we wanted and accepting things as they *are* (even if we continue to work

ACCEPTANCE

on ourselves). Accepting our spouse and the situation as they are allows us to focus on enjoying what we have. (With the caveat that, as we'll cover later, there are some situations that should never be accepted.)

Steps of Acceptance

Let's look at how this plays out, so we can reach the type of acceptance that matters. These steps may not be easy—but they are usually worth it for your well-being and that of your spouse and your marriage.

STEP #1: Realize that change is up to you

Take a deep breath. This may be a hard truth to come to terms with. And frankly, it is a hard truth to write. If your spouse is wrestling with something that is disappointing or even hurtful to you, them, or the marriage, no one can make *them* change. But you have the power to bring about positive change by shifting *you*.

> You have the power to bring about positive change by shifting *you*.

For example, if they are consuming erotica, imagining having sex with someone else, looking at porn, or withholding sexual intimacy, their behavior needs to change. They *should* be taking the responsibility to do so, and you may be desperately wishing for that shift to happen. But the good news is this: While no one can make them change, you are not powerless in the situation.

Whenever we allow something in our spouse to keep us from our own fulfillment, we are choosing to be a type of victim. If they must change before we can be okay, we are trapped by whether they are willing to change. So we try to force change on them, and that usually backfires because humans typically do not respond positively to being pushed.

But when we recognize *our* power to enact change (which includes setting essential boundaries), we step outside of the victim role. Our spouse may or may not be okay with the shift, which is why it may be tempting to keep the status quo. Yet if we want to get unstuck, the process of acceptance described here is *entirely* within our power. (And if you are in a situation where you are being victimized by an unrepentant, wounding spouse, also see the section at the end of the chapter.)

Our realization of that is the first crucial step to getting unstuck and moving forward. We saw this pattern play out strongly in our survey. When the survey-taker was considering a way in which they had a real, ongoing disappointment

ACCEPTANCE

with their spouse as a sexual partner—when something that they were longing for simply wasn't the way they wished (including a lack of sex)—67 percent of our respondents had largely or entirely come to terms with it.[1]

Many people start out with an ideal picture of what they want in a spouse and a sexual partner. And over time they find out that there is a gap: Their spouse is different from their ideal in a particular way (in their physical appearance, way of handling arguments, sexual frequency or practices, etc.) and they probably won't change that much. To what degree have you come to terms with that particular gap between ideal and real? (Choose one.)	
I've largely/entirely come to terms with it.	67%
I've somewhat come to terms with it, but I still struggle a bit.	27%
I haven't yet come to terms with it well.	6%

Source: MIS, n=1097

How did they do that? Fully *90 percent* stated the change was within themselves. *They* were the ones who had shifted. Only 10 percent said the change that allowed for a sense of resolve had come from changes in their spouse.

Their sense of acceptance—coming to terms with the gap between what they wanted versus what was—*really* mattered for their well-being (or lack of it). Those who stated they had not come to terms with that gap were 3.5 times more likely to report a dissatisfying marriage. And those who *had* largely/entirely come to terms with it were nearly 3 times more likely to report being happy in their marriage.[2]

Now, again: Just because acceptance is crucial for moving forward does not mean all characteristics and behaviors should be accepted! Some definitely *should not* be accepted and require an entirely different approach. (More on that on page 211, following the end of this chapter.)

> Just because acceptance is crucial for moving forward does not mean all characteristics and behaviors should be accepted!

That said, most of the things that get couples stuck do need a level of acceptance so change can occur. So how do we get there?

STEP #2: Grieve what is not the way you wished

To fully accept our spouse (which is not the same thing as condoning unhealthy behavior), we must fully release those things about them that negatively distract us. We must grieve and let go of who they are not, if we are to accept who they are.

If you have ever lost a close friend or family member, you know that you have to work through many emotions to accept that you will no longer be able to grab coffee and discuss the

ACCEPTANCE

latest news about work or the kids. But in healthy grieving, you eventually reach full acceptance that this person will never again be part of your life here on earth.

That same process must happen to come to terms with many disappointments in marriage.

We encounter many people who *haven't* grieved the loss of something in their spouse. For example, a wife might say, "I know he's ADHD off the charts, but I need him to really care about what happened during my day. I need him to sit on the couch and just listen." Or a husband might say, "I know she's not a workout-type person, but I really need her to come to the gym with me." Or maybe it is something much more significant. Maybe you are struggling with the loss of your husband's erections after prostate surgery, or the chronic fatigue and pain your wife feels from her autoimmune issues.

If you wish for something you will never have, you're not only going to be distressed, but dissatisfaction with your spouse could grow exponentially. Even worse, you can easily miss what is wonderful about them.

Grieving means you accept that something will *never* be a part of your life.

One man's comment illustrated how he had moved from disappointment in his intimate relationship to true enjoyment. He said, "I dreamt of having a wife who would flash me in the store when no one else was looking. I would have *loved* my wife to be playful and creative and surprise me with her spontaneity. My wife, however, is an amazingly beautiful, competent, and successful woman—in part because she is a bit anxious, precise, and structured. In terms of managing our household and everything else, she is brilliant. But she will never be the playful, spontaneous sex kitten I would love. Don't get me wrong—while a bit routine, our sex life is very enjoyable. We have learned each other well. But I had to accept that she will never drip chocolate syrup on her body and invite me to lick it off."

Once you fully grieve who your spouse is *not*, some amazing dynamics are free to happen.

First, you stop seeing your spouse through a deficit lens, focusing on what they are not. For example, I (Michael) might see a great guy who loves his wife dearly, but his wife sees someone who lacks the Type-A assertiveness she associates with strong masculinity in his work, parenting, and in the bedroom. Rather than appreciating the empathic, caring, pleasing man he is, she is increasingly irritated by him, seeing only his weakness instead of being drawn by his strengths. But if she is able to grieve who he is not, the deficit lens can drop away as she chooses not to focus on it.

Second, fully accepting who our spouse is not allows us to see who they *are*. We tend to do that more easily with our children. If we grieve that they are never going to be the athlete we wanted them to be, we can celebrate the artist they are becoming.

ACCEPTANCE

Finally, once you grieve who your spouse is not, you foreclose on ever having it as a part of your life. In fact, over time, the idea of what you wanted begins to feel *wrong* and weird.

For example, consider the man above who had fully grieved and accepted that his wife would never be a spontaneous sex kitten. Imagine him at work one day, overhearing a co-worker telling her friend she bought chocolate syrup so her husband could lick it off. If that man hadn't grieved the loss of this fantasy, he might now have a risk of wanting to fantasize about his co-worker or going online to search for videos of couples doing it. But if he *has* accepted his chocolate fantasy will never be a part of his life, his experience would be like someone suggesting you run to the coffeeshop to see your deceased friend. It would be *weird*, and definitely not compelling. There might be a twinge of "that *would* have been fun with my wife, if life had gone differently," but there's no real interest today. His co-worker and her fantasy are not a threat.

This is how it is supposed to be in marriage. Marriage is a choice and then a lifelong commitment. The wedding vow phrase "forsaking all others" is an old-fashioned phrase, but it foreshadows the grief process in marriage. It acknowledges, "Not only am I choosing all of who you are and who you are not, I am also actively choosing *not* any other."

STEP #3: Extend grace

By the late 1990s, I (Michael) had fallen in love with working with marriages but was still trying to learn what was effective. In observing premarital couples who were giddy with love alongside crisis couples struggling to be in the same room, I spotted one huge difference between them: a willingness to extend grace.

Grace is often defined as unmerited favor. In marriage we extend grace by choosing to see the best in each other, despite all the very real ways we mess up. It means putting into practice that biblical command we mentioned earlier, to focus on those things that are excellent and worthy of praise rather than the things that are worthy of driving you crazy![3] For example, perhaps you choose to view your spouse as persistent (a trait you love) rather than stubborn (a trait you dislike).

During premarital counseling, one young, extroverted man declared, "She's a strong introvert. I would much rather have gone to the party, but I like how she keeps me grounded. We stayed home and watched a fascinating documentary together." Now that's grace, right? The question is: How does he *keep* that sense of grace so that ten years into marriage, he is just as appreciative—rather than irritated about staying home?

In a lifelong marriage, grace must be a lifelong choice.

ACCEPTANCE

One husband Jeff and I (Shaunti) interviewed described how, after many years of difficulty, he and his wife had in recent years created a beautiful marriage and sex life.

HER: When we got married, it was hard for me to trust. And I was awful. I would fight him *hard*. I was scared of intimacy because of some past abuse. So it has been a long haul, but now it's so different. I feel comfortable walking around naked! And most of that is because my husband has shown me grace over and over again.

HIM: Well . . . not early on. I wanted to talk about sex a lot and wanted to *have* sex a lot. I was very pushy. I was thinking, "This is marriage, this is what we do!" And that's *true*, but me always being disappointed wasn't going to get us anywhere.

I actually came to Christ during this rough period and realized that I couldn't do it by myself. I had to rely on Him. Because I had to be consistent so she could know I was going to always be there. No matter what she said to me, I wasn't going to call her names or turn into a monster. I was going to forgive her. See the good in her. Knowing divorce wasn't an option helped me hang in there—which helped her finally accept that I meant it. I knew this wasn't going to be for a year or five years, but for a lifetime.

HER: He kept showing me grace during the rough patches, and it was finally like, "Wait a minute, there's no reason to fight him because *he's on my side*!" Sex is *totally* different today as a result because he has helped me feel totally secure.

STEP #4: Honor them

After grieving who our spouse is and is not, and extending grace, we can learn to honor them. This is an essential final step for *true* acceptance.

Think about our steps thus far. If you don't **grieve**, then what your spouse is *not* is all you see. It is as if you are standing an inch from a scratched-up porch column; all you see is the column, and most of what fills your eyes are the blemishes.

Having **grace** is like stepping back several yards and refocusing. You can see the whole house—which helps you to not focus on the scratches on the porch column.

Giving **honor**, then, is like looking at the house and realizing it is *beautiful*. Look at those graceful windows! The front door is so welcoming; it makes you want to walk inside.

At the opening of the chapter, we mentioned that our spouse is probably only 80 percent of what we need, with 20

ACCEPTANCE

percent that is very different from what we were hoping for. When you honor your spouse, you focus on and celebrate that 80 percent.

In therapy one day, a higher-desire wife told me (Michael), in a somewhat irritated voice, "I've accepted that having lower desire is just the way my husband is."

"No," I pushed back, "you are *tolerating* it in him. That isn't acceptance. How long will you be able to tolerate it before you crack under the weight of your frustration and shift to resentment?"

Sexuality is so diverse; it is sad when someone gets stuck on one type of behavior their spouse is opposed to or characteristic they don't measure up to. Especially because if you can move through the frustration, there is so much *more* on the other side.

For example, suppose you are an initiating, higher-desire spouse. You have two options. You can try to demand or wish that your spouse have initiating desire when in fact they experience receptive desire—but you will likely begin to experience resentment. *Or* you can grieve that your spouse does not match your desire, extend grace for the impact that has on you and your marriage, and honor the desire they do have.

Honoring your spouse might mean deciding to get curious and going on a voyage of discovery. How does their receptive desire work? What makes it good for them and for your ability to connect? You still hold them in high esteem and seek to learn.

Honor makes acceptance complete. And it allows for true enjoyment. Because once you truly accept that your spouse isn't everything you wanted, you can see and enjoy what you've got.

> Once you truly accept that your spouse isn't everything you wanted, you can see and enjoy what you've got.

On our survey, four in ten of the survey-takers—41 percent—had won through to this sense that they were not only *accepting* those things that were not what they had wished, but were actually *enjoying* their spouse. ("I am enjoying what I've got, and not missing what I don't have.") And the differences between that group and everyone else were striking: 89 percent reported being happy in marriage, compared with just 49 percent of those who were still dealing with disappointment or anger about the situation.

All the way through the survey, those who had come to a more complete sense of acceptance and enjoyment had more positive responses. For example, they were more likely to enjoy being sexually playful than those with middling or

ACCEPTANCE

As you think about your spouse and your sex life, how does your situation differ from your original ideal?

	Total	Happy in Marriage	"Meh" in Marriage	Unhappy in Marriage
I've accepted the situation and am enjoying what I've got and not missing what I don't have	41%	89%	10%	1%
I'm in the middle – I'm mostly accepting of what I have and don't have (but may still be missing it)	37%	67%	30%	3%
I haven't come to terms with it and/or am disappointed/sad/angry about what I'm missing	22%	49%	39%	13%

Source: MIS, n=1097
Question and answer choices are paraphrased and combined from two questions. See research document for specifics.

Happiness in marriage increases with acceptance.

no acceptance. They were more likely to communicate well. They were less likely to hold *themselves* back about mentioning something they might want to try sexually.

And it wasn't because the accepters were always dealing with lesser issues. Many among that group were dealing with one or more significant sex-related physical conditions, had mental health issues, or were in low-sex/no-sex marriages. The path of acceptance can work for everyone.

That said, it doesn't mean it *should* work for everyone. As mentioned earlier, some things should not be accepted, which is addressed in the special note from Michael at the end of this chapter.

What Is Our Next Step?

We recommend two main action items coming out of this challenging chapter. These may not be easy, but they are very important—for your marriage and for you.

First: As you look at the steps of acceptance above, where are you? Be very honest with yourself. Is there something you need to grieve and accept that it will never be part of your life? Do you need to start thinking of having grace with your spouse as a lifetime choice? Or maybe you need to step back even further and wrestle with the concept that change is up to you. Identify what you most need to work on and get started.

Second: If you need outside help to navigate the issues you face, please seek it out. A trained and licensed counselor is most likely to be equipped to help, but even if such a situation isn't available to you—for cost, or other reasons—enlist a supportive and wise mentor. Regardless of which direction you go, find someone who is supportive of both you and your marriage.

As long as you are not in a situation where your spouse is doing great damage to you and unwilling to acknowledge it

ACCEPTANCE

or change, we encourage you to do the work of fully going through the steps above. We would love for you to arrive not just at *acceptance* but *enjoyment* of your spouse and your intimate life. (And if you are in a much more difficult situation, please see the special section starting on page 211.)

We Always Have Hope

We need to accept and grieve what will never be, and let it go. But we live every day with the truth that there is One who can bring dead things to life.

One man I (Michael) worked with had been dissatisfied with his and his wife's intimate life for many years. He was especially frustrated that his wife would not do a particular sex act that made her uncomfortable. He pressured her many times for it, and as he tried to make her into the sexual partner he thought he wanted, he became demanding and selfish.

So he hired a "professional" (me) to tell her she had to change. Professionals have even less influence than spouses, but during counseling he began to realize that he had the power—indeed, the responsibility—to change himself. As he grieved the loss of ever experiencing the sex act he was so focused on, he was finally able to extend his wife grace. That allowed him to begin to honor the sexual partner she was.

His wife began to experience him cherishing her rather than demanding from her. She began to feel safer, which allowed her to become more playful. In time, they developed a rich menu of sexual behaviors they both enjoyed. They had so much fun together he really didn't care that the old behavior wasn't part of the menu.

Which is the way it so often works. What we give up can make room for something that is so much better.

. . . .

A Special Note from Dr. Michael Sytsma:

How far do we push acceptance and grace?

I occasionally encounter someone in a marriage that seems truly intolerable. When an individual is still married because both are seeking to change and serve one another, however imperfectly, I am a confident guide in their process. I am uncomfortable, however, when I learn someone feels trapped in a very damaging marriage. Often, they have heard teaching on divorce that isn't truly biblical, and I walk them through what Scripture actually says. For example, to help them see that tolerating sin *is* sin.

A discussion of biblical teaching on divorce, abuse, and related issues goes beyond the scope of this book.

ACCEPTANCE

We debated whether we should say anything on this matter, knowing that we don't have the room to say everything. Discussion on this topic is fraught and can be misunderstood. But at a minimum, it is crucial to state this directly: Some behaviors and attitudes are wholly unacceptable in relationship.

We hold a high and sacred view of the marital covenant. We also believe that biblically, the sacredness of the individual is greater than the sacredness of the institution. (For example, Mark 2:27.)

This is often very true in the sexual part of marriage. Couples stand at the altar and covenant to be exclusive in their relationship with each other and to honor and serve. Which means grace is often called for in even major violations when the offender is genuinely repentant. But where a spouse is doing great damage to their mate and is completely unwilling to seek change, the marriage covenant might be broken.

It may seem easier to accept that a marriage is broken when there are blatant infidelity violations; it is as if there's a sort of pass for divorce when a spouse is caught in a sexual sin. Yet tolerance is sometimes inappropriately encouraged for pressured sexual behavior in marriage or ongoing ridicule that truly kills the spirit of the wounded spouse.

Ongoing ridicule, physical aggression, sexual acts without consent of both spouses,[4] inviting others into the act, total unilateral withholding of sex in the absence of physical prohibitions or abuse, and other types of damaging sexual behavior in marriage are unacceptable. Change here is required on the part of the violator, not on the part of the wounded. I have worked with too many marriages where one spouse had been regularly raped by the other with the justification that "we are married, so his/her body is mine and I can do with it what I want." I have also seen too many marriages where one spouse simply refuses to engage sexually and will not consider working on it, in total breach of the marital covenant. These examples are totally counter to the heart and command of the example of Christ.

While this type of utterly damaging behavior can occur with either spouse, it is particularly important to mention because of the way God honors women, who historically have been more likely to be the victims of abuse. Among the ancient Israelites, daughters were sometimes given to men of a higher economic status to set them up for a better life. But what if that husband eventually decided he was more enamored by the next pretty young thing to come along? To those who had

ACCEPTANCE

the least rights in their culture, God made a law that if a woman's husband stopped providing provision, protection, and sexual relations, she could divorce him at no cost.[5] God explicitly provided a way out for a wife who was being dishonored in those three rights of marriage.

Does this mean a dishonored wife (or a husband, for that matter) should leave? Not necessarily.[6] And as mentioned earlier, a real discussion is beyond what we can include in this book.

For now, the key is this: If you are in a marriage where your spouse is demeaning and engaging in ridicule, or is demanding or participating in behavior that is abusive or harmful to you, please seek outside guidance. (We also include some resources on our website.) Whether you are told to stay married as a duty or you are told to immediately seek divorce, either extreme may not be grounded. (In cases of imminent threat, though, please create an immediate physical separation for your safety and that of your children.) As you seek counsel, look for someone who will wrestle with you in the difficulty of the decision.

10

a higher view

moving forward with what matters most

A number of years ago, I (Shaunti) was getting ready to speak at a large annual Christian women's event. Backstage, as I waited for my mic check, I asked the organizers a standard question: "Since my talk is about relationships, do you want me to cover the sex topic? I want to be sensitive to whatever is appropriate for your group."

The delightful eighty-one-year-old woman who had started the organization forty years before immediately laughed. "Honey, you know you need to cover that topic!"

One of the other organizers said, "But I think it might make some people uncomfortable—"

The vibrant, white-haired founder cackled. "Let them be uncomfortable! I know the talk is respectful, so it's our own insecurities that are making us uncomfortable. Even at eighty-seven and eighty-one, my husband and I still have insecurities. Just the other day, I was in a Bible study about realizing that we are loved and accepted and beautiful just as we are, with all our imperfections. The teacher suggested that the next time we got out of the shower, we stand proudly in front of the bathroom mirror in all our glory and tell that to ourselves."

She smiled impishly. "So yesterday I dropped the towel, looked straight in the mirror, and asked myself out loud, 'Am I loved, accepted, and beautiful just as I am?!' And I hear a chuckle and turn my head, and there's my husband lying on the bed in the bedroom. And he says, 'Yes you are, and bring it over here, baby!'"

I couldn't help laughing out loud, I loved that anecdote so much. And today, whenever I share that story onstage, everyone has the same reaction as I did: *I want that to be me! I want to have that delightful, playful, intimate life with my spouse when we are in our eighties!*

What was their secret?

In this book, we have covered many tips and research findings on sex and marriage that will help you discover the secrets that matter. But without the topic of this chapter, there will always be a limitation in our intimate life. Because what allowed this couple to have that beautiful intimate life in their eighties is what allows all those tips and research findings to work well to begin with: knowing and living out the ultimate *purpose* of sex.

What Is Sex About?

The primary teaching in culture is that sex is about pleasure. Parts and technique are focused on physical function toward an intense, overwhelming pleasure. If your world doesn't rock, something is not right.

Is sex about pleasure? Clearly, that's part of it! Our bodies are designed for profound sexual pleasure. According to many medical sources, the glans of the sexual organs are among the most sensitive regions in the body. Women have a complex organ designed with no purpose *other* than pleasure! But is pleasure the be-all and end-all?

A primary teaching of the historical church was that sex is about procreation. And clearly, that's also part of it! But given just how profoundly sex encompasses our full body, soul, heart, and relationship, procreation does not seem a complete enough answer. After all, God could have designed a host of other ways for us to procreate. He could have had us follow the example of the fish, where the egg is laid in the bed and fertilized externally. Why do we have the parts we do set up to function the way they do,

CONCLUSION

so we are brought together face-to-face? There's a bigger story here.

A Higher Image

We know a lot about an artist by his or her design. As God designed sex, it is a reflection of Him. As such, *sex is a divine object lesson.*

Sex was designed to teach us about God, about ourselves, about our relationship with each other, and about our relationship with Him. As a mirror reflects your face, at its best, sex reflects who God is. While there are many examples of this, two of them are vital to applying everything we have talked about in this book.

Sex is about yada *intimacy*

The writer of Genesis records that Adam *yada* his wife, Eve, and she bore a son. Typically translated as "knew," the Hebrew word *yada* means "to know."[1] While it would be easy to view the use of *yada* as a euphemism, it is actually a powerful choice of words reflecting God's higher design for sex.

What if in God's original design, the act of sex is about seeking to know, causing to know, entering into and being entered into? Sex becomes about learning one another and exposing our innermost selves fully to one another.

At its fullest, sex is about sharing and creating a profound intimacy with each other—a oneness that often takes years of learning and growth to experience in full. In seeking to experience *yada* sex, we are pursuing a type of intimacy that is unique to a sacred relationship.

Intimacy and oneness are central to God's very nature—and to His heart. In fact, Jesus said His purpose, including being crucified, was *so we can be in intimate relationship with God.*[2] It is not surprising, then, that God says He despises things that disrupt marital intimacy and oneness.

Sex both reflects and fosters great intimacy. As a couple pursues oneness in sex, a vast array of chemicals flood the body, helping us to feel safe and trusting and physiologically connecting us. This is by design.

A couple seeking intimacy and healthy oneness in their marriage is pursuing the heart of God. If the primary goal of sex is oneness, a couple will find themselves in the pursuit of a healthy sex life. If the primary goal is the climax, or any other *part* of sex, sex will always be incomplete, and we will do damage to ourselves and our relationship over time.

A couple seeking intimacy and healthy oneness in their marriage is pursuing the heart of God.

CONCLUSION

But when the primary goal is intimacy *and* oneness, we have the greatest chance of rich sex as well—even as we age. When body parts are no longer the focus, they do not have to work perfectly to have intimacy. One of my (Michael's) clients told me that at age seventy-four, "I am having the best sex of my life even though my penis doesn't always show up for the party." How? Because he has learned to be focused on intimacy first. Arousal and orgasm, while important, become the fruit of the process, not the point. Their absence does not destroy either the process or the goal.

It is heartbreaking and unnecessary when I see my clients give up being sexual with each other because of a physical issue. Now, as we have urged earlier, if there is pain or dysfunction, stepping away from intercourse may be important while the couple problem-solves. But if intimacy is the goal, many other sexual activities can be pursued. I encourage such couples to triple the sexual, sensual touch they share with each other. This is not only doable, but important in the pursuit of intimacy.

Which points us to a second crucial aspect of this higher view of sex.

Sex is about both body and spirit—it is "incarnational"

If someone were to say that Jesus Christ was fully God, but He wasn't man like we are, a follower of the Christian faith would say, "No, that is inaccurate teaching—heresy." You cannot remove the physicality of Jesus and still have Him be Christ.

In similar fashion, if we said He was probably the best man to have ever lived, but He wasn't God, a Christ follower would reject this as well. You cannot remove the divinity of Jesus and have Him still be Christ. He is fully God *and* fully man. It takes both to be Christ. This principle is called *incarnation*.

At its fullest, sex reflects the incarnate. It is designed to be totally about both the *body* and the *spirit* of the act.

Historically, the church has often overemphasized the spirit of the act. For many years, scholars taught that Song of Solomon was solely a divine allegory of Christ's love for his bride. Certainly, in no way could a description of the tasting of her garden or his fruit[3] be about oral sex! Heavens, no! God would never speak of something as base as physical pleasure, right?

Except . . . a plain reading of the text shows that it is about *both* the spirit of the act *and* a loving couple engaging in sex.

Conversely, culture often emphasizes only the body of the act. Sex becomes entertainment—a sport. It's all about parts and technique and how you play the game for the win—the greatest pleasure. At its extreme, this view holds that attending to heart and relationship is quite unnecessary—or even creates distractions or obstacles to pleasure or fulfilment.

Except . . . just focusing on the body of the act does great damage to the individual and the relationship when the spirit of the act is absent.

For sex to be complete and truly great, it must be incarnate—fully body and fully spirit. If either spouse focuses *just* on the physical of the act (i.e., bigger, better orgasms without caring for how the behavior impacts their spouse's heart), the greater meaning of the act is at risk of being torn apart, and sex becomes disincarnate. Or if either spouse focuses *just* on the spirit of the act (for example, "I'd rather never have sex again, I just want to be close"), sex is missing a key component and becomes disincarnate. Either way, the act of sex is now incomplete, not whole, unbalanced. Over time, this distorted type of sex will run out of energy, wither, and do damage in the relationship.

Now, it is perfectly okay for a spouse to *emphasize* one side or the other. The key is for *both* spouses to appreciate and embrace the focus of the *other*. To accept influence from each other and fight to keep sex about both the body and the spirit. Let's give you an example.

Consider Sam: He is the high-desire spouse and is often focused on the *body* of the act. He wants to engage sexually with his wife, Jasmine. When he initiates, she often responds in a way that says, "We can do that after you touch my heart." She is asking for the *spirit* of the act. After Sam takes her on a date and attends to her heart, Jasmine wants to engage physically.

While they emphasized different aspects, they accepted influence from each other. They worked to keep sex about both the body and the spirit—they worked to keep it incarnate.

We talk with many couples who focus on the body without attending to the spirit. Sex is just about what they do to each other and what they want done to them. The focus is on the technique or how to get their spouse to behave the way they want. It's just an act they do rather than an event that rises out of their love for each other. We grieve whenever we hear of marriages in which one spouse is demanding access to the other, believing it's their "right." They have totally lost focus on the spirit of the act.

But the reverse shows up just as often.

"I'm not really into sex," one wife told me (Michael). "It doesn't really feel good to me. I love my husband and know it's important to him, though, so I do it at least once a week. And I usually feel more connected after, so it's fine." While I appreciate her desire to please him and that she experiences and enjoys the connection—both of which *are* reflective of the spirit of the act—she is sacrificing her own experience of the body of the act. This, too, is disincarnate. Their sex life is likely to become increasingly unhealthy—all because neither of them fought for their sex life to be about body and spirit for both of them.

While keeping her heart open to the spirit of the connection, this couple could *also* nurture the body of the act by prioritizing an effort to discover what it would take for sex to be physically enjoyable to her. Similarly, and ironically, as he invites her to prioritize the body of the act for her, he is actually caring for her spiritually.

If couples don't fight to keep sex incarnational, one or both spouses will eventually get hurt, and their sex life will falter. So if you realize one of you is not experiencing *both* the body and the spirit of the act, please step back, discuss what is missing, and commit to making it rich for both.

An Intimate Future

Making sex good for both partners, and full in both body and spirit, is the ultimate goal of this book. The richest sexual intimacy occurs when we learn our spouse and reflect the heart of God. When we pursue *yada* intimacy and keep it about both the body and spirit. When we focus not primarily on following rules or figuring out what the church and others *say* is right, but first and foremost trying to be like Him.

> The richest sexual intimacy occurs when we learn our spouse and reflect the heart of God.

We hope that what you have learned in this book has given you a glimpse of the great vision for your intimate life and how you can get there. So be curious and explore each other. Don't just accept your assumptions. Talk through the points in this book. And enjoy spending the rest of your marriage on the process of discovery. The journey may not always be easy, but it will be rich and well worth it.

We'll leave you with this conversation from a couple we interviewed along the way. A couple who, when we asked, said they wanted to give an interview because "We want to give the perspective of a happy couple who got married at age twenty, has been married forty years, and is really enjoying sex. We want to encourage couples that this is totally possible."

HER: We got married so young, and we were probably pretty selfish. We *thought* we knew what we were doing, but we really didn't. So there was a lot of fumbling.

HIM: But actually . . . I think "fumbling" could be redefined as "learning together." We had to learn each other in every way. Originally, we wanted the Hollywood version of a perfect sex life. But authenticity is far more important than perfection. We learned you have to completely trust this other person. You trust that they have your best interest in mind.

That they accept you for what you look like, and who you are. *Then* you are able to be authentic and respond well. And that really only comes when you put God at the center of everything, to live in that sacrificial love the Bible talks about. *That* is what creates the mutual, intimate experience that every marriage is going for.

acknowledgments

Hundreds of people contributed to this book and the Marriage Intimacy Project. Since a full accounting would run for twenty pages and would still miss someone, allow us to simply say a heartfelt "thank you" to everyone who helped make this project happen.

The contributions of some individuals have been particularly crucial.

Joint Acknowledgments

Most important, Jeff Feldhahn was the silent partner in this entire project. He was at every meeting, was deeply involved in all the research, and his leadership and insight are foundational to everything you have read here.

Gathering and analyzing the data for the Marriage Intimacy Project (MIP) was an undertaking of immense scope. We are especially grateful to the silent donors who funded and encouraged this research. We are also thankful for the thousands of people who sat for interviews or participated in surveys, and for the help, encouragement, skill, advice, and the vast number of hours spent by advisors, partners, and team members—both on the MIP and to keep everything running in our organizations.

We must especially acknowledge Calvin Edwards for the many hours helping us shape the content and survey data, and our amazing Bethany House editor, Andy McGuire, who probably never expected his research-based past to land him in an advisory role on *this* topic! Deep thanks also to Baker Publishing/Bethany House president/CEO Dwight Baker, and the other Baker/Bethany leaders and editors who shaped and supported this book and its messaging, especially Sharon Hodge, Mark Rice, Deirdre Close, and Heather Adams of Choice Media.

On Shaunti's team, our joint thanks to: Charlyn Elliott for managing a vast number of operational details and yet again being our amazing spreadsheet-and-chart Jedi Master. Eileen Kirkland for the hours arranging research events and interviews and valiantly protecting Shaunti's writing time, even if it meant rescheduling a podcast for the fourth time. Deanna Hamilton and Tally Whitehead for tackling any analysis/research project needed. Debbie Mason for helping us set up so much of the research and designing the resources surrounding it, and Samantha Griggs for jumping in at the deep end as we created application resources.

On the statistical side, we thank Aubrey Gold for her initial development and analysis with this project, Bud Sanders for his statistical investigation and analysis, and Stephanie Greene for her help with the number crunching. We especially thank Morgen Feldhahn for her SPSS and statistical analysis skills, and courage in tackling a college internship on this topic . . . with her parents.

Our gratitude also goes to our professional survey company partners, whose rigorous efforts delivered high-quality data—especially Felicia Rogers and Julie Trujillo at Decision Analyst and Kin Parikh at Dynata.

An immense number of people were involved in the early research. We are extremely grateful for the help of the dozens of pastors, staff, and volunteers of the diverse churches that served as our research sites: Cornerstone Church, Fuquay-Varina, NC; Ephrata Community Church, Ephrata, PA; Fellowship Bible Church, Topeka, KS; Harvest Christian Fellowship, Orange County, CA; Mountain West Church, Stone Mountain, GA; and Victory World Church, Norcross, GA. We are also grateful for author friends (Jill and Mark Savage, Greg and Julie Gorman, Apryl and Ozzie Ortiz) who helped us conduct pilot surveys among their followers.

Deep thanks to the team at the American Association of Christian Counselors for their partnership in doing research among leaders and creating resources for them: especially Tim Clinton, Ben Allison, Kyle Sutton, Garrett Hedrick, and Mercy Connors.

Special thanks to Lucy and Kene Iloenyosi of Neatworks, Inc., for yet another beautiful cover and brand design.

Acknowledgments from Michael

First, my deepest thanks go to my wife, Karen, for her grace in life—and as I worked on this project. To our sons, Josiah and Caleb, and Caleb's new wife, Dinah—may your marriages be a bit better because of what I have passed on. To my parents, Rev. Ronald and Carol Sytsma: Thank you for always believing in and praying for me.

Deep gratitude to the thousands of clients who courageously share their stories with me that I might learn. You've been gracious in letting me into sacred spaces, and I honor your stories and work.

To the many who helped shape my learning and influenced this book, I am indebted. I am grateful to my friend and mentor Dr. Douglas Rosenau, whom we all miss. Your legacy lives on. Thanks to the amazing sex therapists and special friends whose input was critical in this book, including Debra Taylor, PsyD, LMFT, CST; Angela Landry, LMFT,

CST; and Marti Witherow, PhD, LPC, LMFT, CST; you ladies rock! To Christy Christopher for your valuable time, coaching, input, and encouragement. And thanks to the courageous team who joined me as founding professors for the Institute for Sexual Wholeness, and were the iron that sharpened iron: Cliff and Joyce Penner, Jim Childerston, Mark Yarhouse, Christopher McCluskey, and Diane Langberg. Also Mark Laaser and William Cutrer, who finished their race well.

To the Building Intimate Marriages team, thanks for your grace and for keeping things running while I was otherwise distracted. Thanks to "Bad Company" and the men who keep me focused, help problem-solve, listen, and make me better.

Finally, thanks to Shaunti and Jeff for inviting me on this journey. You have helped me articulate what I have learned and provided a platform for some of my soapboxes. You sought to learn this subject well, always staying curious. I am impressed by the countless hours spent in the research and your insistence on excellence. You have been awesome students, partners, and guides.

Acknowledgments from Shaunti

Jeff and I must start by acknowledging Michael: We are so honored you joined us in this project. It has been an exceptional experience to learn from your outstanding therapy and research skills. It has also been a joy to work with you . . . despite the fact that you enjoy using anatomically correct terms and watching us squirm.

I'm grateful for the amazing current and former team members who not only contributed to the MIP and the book, but kept courses, blogs, and everything else running when I was so focused on this project—and who supported me through my bout with breast cancer in the middle of it. In addition to those mentioned above, our deep thanks go to Amy Masaschi, Suzanne Stewman, and Laura Warner (all of whom helped in various research projects), as well as Katie Phillips, Beth Peazzoni, Nicole Owens, Laura Banks, Dana Ashley, and Caroline Niziol. All of us are grateful for and miss Naomi Duncan, who began the project with us before she went Home.

I'm also very grateful for my prayer partners and prayer team, who truly did the "real work" behind the scenes, especially my praying sisters, Kristin Jordan and Ruth Okediji.

Many leaders with a specialty in this topic encouraged, educated, and advised me. Special thanks to Juli Slattery, Jennifer Degler, J Parker, Bonny Burns, Chris Taylor, and Gaye Christmus for sharing their wisdom. Thanks also to Julie Fidler and to several anonymous women from the trauma/abuse/neurodiverse marriage community for the hours spent sharing information, answering questions, and helping me keep in mind those who are most hurting.

My family has been amazing through it all. To Judy Reidinger: I'm so grateful for you, Mom. Thank you for everything from constantly making dinner so Jeff and I could keep writing, to doing data entry. To our daughter, Morgen: You are *really good* at data analytics, we are so proud of you, and yes, we will pay for your therapy after this project. To our son, Luke: We are proud of you too! Thanks for your constant help . . . and for putting up with three of the four members of the family talking about sex nonstop for three years. To Jeff: You are the secret weapon in all of this. Thanks for your amazing willingness to do *everything* for the family, for all your work behind the scenes, and for being the most amazing man I know.

Finally, and most importantly, this project was only possible because of the One who is the true Author of all. The prayer shared by all of us—Shaunti, Jeff, Michael, and our entire team—is that this book would draw married couples closer to each other, and closer to Him.

our methodology
and research process

the marriage intimacy project study

This appendix is published online
at secretsofsexandmarriage.com.

notes

Chapter 1: What We Want—And How to Get There

1. Throughout this book, all names and identifying details have been changed. Original quotes may have been edited or combined for clarity.

2. Laquitta Walker and Danielle Taylor, "Same-Sex Couple Households: 2019," U.S. Census Bureau, February 2021, https://www.census.gov/content/dam/Census/library/publications/2021/acs/acsbr-005.pdf.

3. Throughout the book, we note wherever data includes only mixed-sex couples; otherwise, it includes all respondents. See a basic analysis of the data from same-sex, bisexual, and non-binary marriages and individuals at our website.

Chapter 2: What Are Married Couples Up to in the Bedroom?

1. Marcel D. Waldinger et al., "A Multinational Population Survey of Intravaginal Ejaculation Latency Time," *Journal of Sexual Medicine* 2, no. 4 (July 2005): 492–7.

2. Premature ejaculation (males experiencing orgasm too quickly) is a common problem, but typically only diagnosed when the orgasm happens within sixty seconds.

3. David L. Rowland et al., "Orgasmic Latency and Related Parameters in Women During Partnered and Masturbatory Sex," *Journal of Sexual Medicine* 15, no. 10 (October 2018):1463–1471.

4. All data in Wrong Assumption #1 is from the Matched Pair Survey (MPS) unless otherwise noted.

5. On MPS, 16 percent of those attending church weekly or more were in low-sex/no-sex marriages, compared with 30 percent of those who rarely or never attended church (only a few times per year, on special occasions, or not at all).

6. On the MIS, 21 percent of couples were in low-sex/no-sex marriages—slightly less than the 23 percent on the MPS.

7. When excluding those who said their low/no-sex status was purely temporary (such as a deployed spouse), 77 percent of low/no-sex respondents described physical or unavoidable reasons such as physical absence, erectile dysfunction or impacts from cancer, menopause or trauma, while 23 percent described choices and issues that were more avoidable, such as a lack of interest in pursuing available solutions, a busy life, or lack of desire due to relational struggles or not expecting pleasure.

8. These two numbers don't total 78 percent due to rounding.

9. Data in these two paragraphs is based on MPS, among mixed-sex couples, excluding marriages declared low/no-sex by both partners. "Most of the time" combines those who "perform oral sex" on their spouse "Always/Almost Always" and "Usually"; "Some of the time" combines "Often" and "Occasionally"; and "Rarely or Never" combines those two answers.

10. Why women have lower rates of orgasm than men is a debated subject. There are likely many factors at work (which cannot be primarily about male-female interaction, since lower rates occur even in lesbian relationships). For example, our data showed in couples reporting poor sexual communication, wives were 15 times more likely to report having orgasms never/almost never compared to couples in marriages with good sexual communication. See secretsofsexandmarriage.com for more information.

11. Talia Shirazi et al., "Women's Experience of Orgasm During Intercourse: Question Semantics Affect Women's Reports and Men's Estimates of Orgasm Occurrence," *Archives of Sexual Behavior* 47, no. 3 (April 2018): 605–613.

12. Kim Wallen and Elisabeth Lloyd, "Female Sexual Arousal: Genital Anatomy and Orgasm in Intercourse," *Hormones and Behavior* 59, no. 5 (May 2011): 780–792.

13. While on the high end, this percentage is in line with other research on sexual pain in men (Seth N. P. Davis, Yitzchak M. Binik, and Serge Carrier, "Sexual Dysfunction and Pelvic Pain in Men: A Male Sexual Pain

Disorder?" *Journal of Sex & Marital Therapy* 35, no. 3 [April 2009]: 182–205) and slightly higher than most studies report for women (Andrew T. Goldstein, Caroline F. Pukall, and Irwin Goldstein, eds., *Female Sexual Pain Disorders: Evaluation and Management*, 2nd ed. [Wiley, 2020].)

14. Andrew T. Goldstein, Caroline F. Pukall, and Irwin Goldstein, eds., *Female Sexual Pain Disorders: Evaluation and Management*, 2nd ed. (Wiley, 2020).

15. Allen S. Gordon et al., "Characteristics of Women with Vulvar Pain Disorders: Responses to a Web-Based Survey," *Journal of Sex and Marital Therapy* 29, Suppl 1 (2003): 45–58. doi:10.1080/713847126.

16. Fear, anxiety, and negative beliefs about sex (for example, due to trauma) are possible causes for vaginismus. But there are other causes for vaginismus and it is not the most common sexual pain. Due to the complexity and myriad of possible diagnoses for sexual pain, a multidisciplinary medical team needs to be involved.

17. Debra is a long-time leader in the sex therapy field. See https://DebraLTaylortherapy.com/.

18. "Couple frequency satisfaction" created as follows for MIS and used for all discussions of frequency satisfaction on MIS. Based on the report of the survey-taking spouse of *their own* and *their spouse's* levels of frequency satisfaction on a 10-point scale: If *both* spouses were 8–10, they were labeled "happy." If *either* spouse was 1–3, they were labeled "unhappy." The remaining spouses (most saying 4–7) were labeled as "meh," or a middling level of frequency satisfaction.

19. Unless otherwise noted, data in the Wrong Assumption #2 and #3 sections is from MIS.

20. Among those with no mental health condition, 75 percent were at the highest level of marital happiness, compared with 66.5 percent of those with mood disorders, and 58 percent of those with trauma or other issues.

21. For simplicity, this chart compares only those with mood disorders to those with no mental health issues, and leaves out other mental health issues, such as trauma.

22. On MPS, among those who answered 1–7 on the 10-point happiness-with-frequency scale, 76 percent said their spouses reported a 1–7 level of happiness with the frequency as well.

23. MPS, mixed-sex couples only. For the purpose of this book, we define "equal desire" as both partners on the MPS reporting the same desired frequency of sex or an individual on the MIS reporting that they and their spouse have equal desire. "Similar desire" is defined as being only one or

two time-slots apart. (Time-slots identified on the "How often would you like sex?" chart on page 113.)

24. A primary axiom in systemic communication theory as articulated by Paul Watzlawick, Janet Beavin Bavelas, and Don D. Jackson, "Some Tentative Axioms of Communication" in *Pragmatics of Human Communication: A Study of Interactional Patterns, Pathologies, and Paradoxes* (New York: W. W. Norton 1967).

25. Adjustments to the communication question on the MIS were conservative. Respondents were moved out of the top answer (they and spouse talk about sex well without any awkwardness or difficulty) if there was a *clear* contradiction in answers to one of five other questions. They were moved into either the "we talk but it can be difficult" bucket or the "we probably avoid talking" bucket depending on the answer. This more realistic measurement is called Adjusted Communication and used hereafter except where otherwise noted. For MIS only and is not relevant to the Matched Pair Survey, which uses the Dyadic Sexual Communication Scale (DSCS) and is not adjusted.

26. Reported level of communication on MPS as assessed by DSCS couple score.

27. On MPS. Based on answers to DSCS.

28. While most who are unhappy with frequency are not great at communication, 41 percent of those who were happy in their marriages did communicate (even if awkwardly), compared with only 14 percent of those who were unhappy in their marriages.

29. Initial analysis indicated more goodwill in the answers of those who talk well about sex versus those who do not, on multiple questions on the survey. This is another area for further study.

30. Among those who said they would have something to share. (Excludes the 29 percent of respondents who said this did not apply because their spouse always satisfied them sexually.)

31. At lovetakeslearning.com you can find an inexpensive, empirically supported program to do at home that is excellent for helping couples learn how to communicate effectively.

Chapter 3: What We See

1. Dr. Dan Simons and Dr. Christopher Chabris conducted the experiment for a Harvard University course they taught. See https://www.youtube.com/watch?v=vJG698U2Mvo.

2. Short documentary, "The Invisible Gorilla, featuring Daniel Simons," 2011; Beckman Institute, University of Illinois, https://www.youtube.com /watch?v=UtKt8YF7dgQ.

3. Shaunti Feldhahn, *The Surprising Secrets of Highly Happy Marriages* (Colorado Springs: Multnomah, 2013), 47.

4. On the MPS, in every category, survey-takers cared more about their spouse having an orgasm than whether they themselves had one. For example, 78 percent said it was quite/very important to them that their spouse climaxed, but only 57 percent placed that importance on it for themselves.

5. On MIS, only 16 percent had what might be termed a "selfish" motivation for doing something nice (like a neck massage) in the hopes of getting lucky.

6. Katherine Gotham, Alison Marvin, et al., "Characterizing the daily life, needs, and priorities of adults with ASD from Interactive Autism Network data," *Autism* 19, no. 7 (October 2015): 794 -804. Of those who self-reported (as opposed to those with guardians and other legal representatives), 73 percent were high-functioning enough to not be diagnosed with autism spectrum disorder (ASD) until after age eighteen; most (65 percent) received Asperger's syndrome as their initial ASD diagnosis. Of this self-reporting group, 80 percent lived with others and 47 percent of those (37.6 percent of the total) lived with a spouse or partner. See also https://www.ncbi.nlm.nih.gov/pmc/articles/PMC4581903/.

7. MIS. Heterosexual respondents.

8. Hebrews 13:4.

9. "283. amiantos," *Thayer's Greek Lexicon* at Biblehub.com, https:// biblehub.com/thayers/283.htm.

10. Leviticus 10:1–3.

11. Proverbs 5:17.

12. See secretsofsexandmarriage.com for recommendations.

13. Matthew 6:22–23.

14. Philippians 4:8

Chapter 4: You Are Not Broken

1. This type of desire has been given different labels, including "assertive desire" (the label Michael used in his dissertation and Shaunti used in earlier books), and "spontaneous desire." Today, Michael prefers "initiating desire," because it better reflects a main distinction (pursuit toward) and because "spontaneous" is an inaccurate depiction of the neurobiology.

There's nothing spontaneous about any type of desire—it is always catalyzed by something.

2. On *both* MIS and MPS, 41 percent of total heterosexuals had initiating desire, saying what is most characteristic of them is "I initiate sexual activity with my spouse because I am in the mood" (MIS) or "I tend to be in the mood for sex and want to pursue it with my spouse" (MPS).

3. MPS, mixed-sex couples. Unless otherwise noted, all data in this chapter is drawn from MPS and, because our focus here is desire patterns across genders, from mixed-sex couples.

4. This is the typical *felt* experience, although on a purely physical level it isn't quite that clean.

5. And can even become abusive.

Chapter 5: "I Want You to Want Me"

1. Calculated based on how often each spouse said they would like to have sex. (MPS)

2. Fifty-one percent of a convenience sample of 150 matched-pair couples.

3. We are really simplifying this. To be more accurate we would say fuel<u>s</u> (plural) because the complex engine of sexual desire actually runs on multiple types of fuel.

4. These numbers can vary greatly from study to study, depending on how desire is defined. We defined it in several different ways that can be explored in the research document available through secretsofsexandmarriage.com.

5. This is consistent with Michael's dissertation and other research that typically finds 20–25 percent of wives as higher desire. (MPS)

6. "Substantial" is defined as being *more than two time-categories apart* on our frequency scale, which you can see in the "How often would you like sex?" chart. For example, if one spouse wanted sex three to four times a week and their partner wanted sex two to three times a month, that is a three time-category gap. (MPS, mixed-sex couples only.)

7. For mixed-sex couples on MPS, 75 percent of husbands and 55 percent of wives stated they wished for more sex than was happening, with 21 percent of husbands and 28 percent of wives saying their desire was essentially equal to what was happening. On the MIS, 63 percent of men wanted more and 32 percent said their desire was equal to what was happening, while 50 percent of women wanted more and 36 percent said their desire was equal to what was happening.

8. MPS, heterosexual only; "less-than-happy" means rating 1–7 on a 10-point scale. (In our study, 8–10 is always labeled "happy," 4–7 is always middling, and 1–3 is "unhappy.")

9. Based on initial analysis. More in-depth research and analysis are needed to determine how impactful the trend is.

10. A "yes" in moving forward from both parties is critical (consent). Not honoring consent has a high cost, which may range from deeply wounding the safety in the relationship to legal action. Either spouse performing sexual acts on the other without consent is defined as marital rape.

11. 1 Thessalonians 4:3–8.

12. As one study concluded, "[W]e have demonstrated that the loss of sexual activity is characterized by relatively reduced testosterone levels, and that its resumption can restore this endocrine pattern." See E. Jannini et al., "Lack of Sexual Activity from Erectile Dysfunction Is Associated with a Reversible Reduction in Serum Testosterone," *International Journal of Andrology* 22, no. 6 (December 1999): 385 -392, https://onlinelibrary.wiley .com/doi/full/10 .1046 /j .1365 -2605 .1999 .00196 .x See also https://www .nature.com/articles/3900832.

Chapter 6: Sexual Healing

1. Meghan Overdeep, "Video of Texas A&M Kicker's Family Watching [. . .]," *Southern Living*, October 12, 2021, https://www.southernliving .com/news/texas-a-m-kicker-seth-small-alabama-family-video.

2. *Cinderella*, Walt Disney Studios, 2015, https://www.imdb.com/title /tt1661199/

3. Adrian Paul Diongzon, "Cinderella 2015 (Escape from the Palace) (Part 1)" 1:54, July 3, 2015, https://www.youtube.com/watch?v=i0-eVfqLY0A.

4. You can find that data, and all the other data referenced in this book, at secretsofsexandmarriage.com. Note that the older data and findings presented have been consistently backed up by newer studies.

5. MIS survey. Includes all orientations. See research document for the detailed data.

6. This is the memorable title of a Kevin Leman book.

7. Angie Landry is co-founder of Restoration Counseling. See www .restorationcounselingtn.com/.

8. This "manipulative" behavior is *not* automatically negative. Manipulation is not inherently bad. The question is: Are we each truly caring for the other? In this case, both spouses felt positive about the process and the outcome.

9. M. Murphy et al., "Changes in Oxytocin and Vasopressin Secretion During Sexual Activity in Men," *Journal of Clinical Endocrinology and Metabolism* 65, no. 4 (October 1987): 738–41.

Chapter 7: The Magic Touch

1. Albert Einstein, Alice Calaprice, ed., *The Ultimate Quotable Einstein* (Princeton, NJ: Princeton University Press, 2010), 20.

2. *Spider-Man*, directed by Sam Raimi, 2002, Columbia Pictures Industries, Inc.

3. Unless otherwise noted, all survey data in this chapter is from MIS, all respondents.

4. Determining how much certain benefits are caused by curiosity rather than simply related to it requires more research.

5. Stephen Covey, *The 7 Habits of Highly Effective People: Powerful Lessons in Personal Change* (United Kingdom: Simon & Schuster, 2013).

Chapter 8: Getting Started

1. All data in this chapter is from MIS.

Chapter 9: Love the One You're With

1. All data in this chapter is from MIS.

2. 2.9 times.

3. Philippians 4:8.

4. Examples of this would include a lifestyle of unrepentant use of porn, other extramarital sexual stimulation (e.g., strip clubs, online sexual/emotional relationships), demanding acts offensive to the spouse, and chronic masturbation.

5. Exodus 21:10.

6. Read the book of Hosea for an example.

Chapter 10: A Higher View

1. Robert L. Thomas, *New American Standard Exhaustive Concordance, Updated Edition: Hebrew-Aramaic and Greek Dictionaries*, Logos Research Edition (Foundation Publications, 1998).

2. John 17:20–21.

3. Song of Solomon 4:16 and 2:3.

Shaunti Feldhahn received her graduate degree from Harvard University and was an analyst on Wall Street before becoming a social researcher, bestselling author, and popular speaker. Today, Shaunti investigates eye-opening truths that change lives and relationships. Her groundbreaking research-based books, many written or researched with her husband, Jeff, have sold nearly 3 million copies in twenty-five languages—for example, *For Women Only*, *For Men Only*, and *Thriving in Love & Money*. Shaunti's findings are regularly featured in the media and widely used in homes, churches, businesses, and counseling centers worldwide. Subscribe to Shaunti's blog at shaunti.com for relationship research and tips.

Facebook: @ShauntiFeldhahn
Instagram: shauntifeldhahn
Twitter: @ShauntiFeldhahn

Dr. Michael Sytsma is a leading sex therapist, pastor, and popular speaker who is passionate about helping couples grow in marriage. He is a licensed professional counselor, certified sex therapist, and an ordained minister with the Wesleyan Church. Michael received his PhD from the University of Georgia specializing in marital sexual therapy, and fell in love with research development and analysis. His original research dissertation was "Sexual Desire Discrepancy in Married Couples." Dr. Sytsma is co-founder of Sexual Wholeness and founder and senior therapist at Building Intimate Marriages. He and his wife, Karen, have been married since 1985 and have two sons. Connect with Dr. Michael Sytsma at intimatemarriage.org and sexualisveritas.com.

Facebook: @DrSytsma
Instagram: BuildingIntimateMarriages
Twitter: @DrSytsma

You May Also Like . . .

Understand one another in the other big issue in marriage: MONEY! Over 90 percent of couples experience some level of tension around money. In fact, it's the number one stressor in relationships. Based on original research, Shaunti and Jeff Feldhahn provide the answers and insights you need to deepen your understanding of each other, leading to clear communication, peace as a couple, and better financial decision-making.

Thriving in Love and Money

BETHANYHOUSE

Stay up to date on your favorite books and authors with our free e-newsletters. Sign up today at bethanyhouse.com.

 facebook.com/BHPnonfiction

 @bethany_house

 @bethany_house_nonfiction

Discover the Truth
He *Wants* You to Know

For Women Only offers fascinating insights into the hidden lives of men. Based upon a landmark nationwide poll, Shaunti Feldhahn offers groundbreaking information and advises how to convert her findings into practical application.

Finally.
You *Can* Understand Her

What makes her tick? What is she really asking (but not actually saying)? Take the guesswork out of trying to please your wife or girlfriend and begin loving her in the way she needs. Easily. *For Men Only* is a straightforward map that will lead you straight into her heart.

**Read an excerpt from this book and more at
www.WaterBrookMultnomah.com**